Edited by Meg Yamamoto
Cover design by Jazmin Welch
Interior design by Sydney Barnes
Photography by Jules Sherred

CATALOGUING DATA AVAILABLE FROM LIBRARY AND ARCHIVES CANADA
ISBN 9781771513968 (softcover)
ISBN 9781771513975 (electronic)

TouchWood Editions acknowledges that the land on which we live and work is within the traditional territories of the Lkwungen (Esquimalt and Songhees), Malahat, Pacheedaht, Scia'new, T'Sou-ke and W̱SÁNEĆ (Pauquachin, Tsartlip, Tsawout, Tseycum) peoples.

We acknowledge the financial support of the Government of Canada through the Canada Book Fund and of the Province of British Columbia through the Book Publishing Tax Credit.

This book was produced using FSC®-certified, acid-free papers, processed chlorine free, and printed with soya-based inks.

Printed in China

27 26 25 24 23   1 2 3 4 5

To six-year-old me and to the six-year-old in everyone who wasn't allowed to live authentically. You are seen and celebrated.

If you really want to make a friend, go to someone's house and eat with [them]. . . .
The people who give you their food give you their heart.
—Cesar Chavez

FOREWORD

"The joy of cooking."

When Jules Sherred says he missed the joy of cooking, I *get* that. On a deep, personal level.

The joy of cooking's not just the title of a ubiquitous cookbook; it's an actual, honest-to-goodness *emotion*. *The feels*, as the kids say. *All the feels*.

I've been the primary meal maker in my little family for several years now. Once my hobbies (cartooning and gaming) became full-time jobs, I needed new ways to spend my downtime.

Cooking was one of them.

I also get Jules's love for Urvashi Pitre's butter chicken (you'll see what I'm talking about a couple of pages from now). What I *didn't* get, at least when I first encountered (and was blown away by) this now viral recipe, was that it was an absolute game changer for those with disabilities.

Growing up relatively privileged, and blissfully free from pain and mobility or other issues, I never once thought about the difficulties others might face in the kitchen, even for what I thought were relatively simple tasks. I'm sorry to say it took Jules and others to help me realize that the friendly confines of the kitchen (my happy place) might be inaccessible to many people.

I've followed Jules on Twitter (for non-cooking reasons—we're both geeks at heart) for many years. However, I was fascinated by his *Disabled Kitchen* posts in particular. Here was an entirely new (to privileged me) side of cooking that I was, frankly, ashamed I'd never considered.

I wanted to learn more.

There are difficult topics discussed in the pages of *Crip Up the Kitchen*, to be sure, but the payoff for me was (along with mouth-watering new recipes) a new way of thinking about the food we eat, where it comes from, its cultural implications, and—in the end—the *deliciousness* of it all.

Crip Up the Kitchen is packed with both common-sense and *uncommon*-sense approaches to meal prep and production. There's so much ridiculously useful information here that it's sure to become a staple in many households. I may even try my hand at canning thanks to this book!

Crip Up the Kitchen is a terrific read. It's full of fabulous, varied recipes from around the world, bursting with mindful discussions of nourishment, nutrition, and accessibility by an assured chef.

I came for the food. I stayed for the food for thought.

John Kovalic
Madison, Wisconsin
February 2022

John Kovalic is an award-winning cartoonist, writer, and cook. He has illustrated games such as Munchkin *and* Apples to Apples, *created the comic strip* Dork Tower, *and, in a previous life, wrote on food and restaurants for Madison's morning newspaper, the* State Journal.

INTRODUCTION

WHY THE INSTANT POT
AND THESE RECIPES?

I will never forget the day I stumbled across Urvashi Pitre's video for her version of butter chicken. I was *incensed*. Why had no one, not a single person, told me what the Instant Pot could do? How it would radically transform my life and my kitchen? Why did they only say "You need one" and then complain about it? *Incensed*!

There was a time when I couldn't cook, and I hated it. Before that time, there was another time when I would happily spend hours cooking. It was nothing for me to spend five hours making my favourite Indian food, which is also comfort food. It brought me so much joy and pleasure. Then, as my neuropathic pain moved to every part of my body, it became increasingly difficult. Then it became a physical impossibility.

Not only did I miss the joy of cooking, but I could no longer eat food I enjoyed. Finding prepared meals that I liked and that met my dietary needs was so much effort. Eating became a chore. I hated the kitchen and every single second I spent in it.

And then I saw Urvashi cook. Then I watched her some more. Then I learned she had arthritis, which my neuropathic pain mimics, resulting in a 20-year misdiagnosis. And then—*incensed* because nobody told me!

After spending weeks watching every one of her videos, I became confident enough to think, "I can do this." Not only in terms of mobility but also in terms of overcoming my fears about my kitchen blowing up as I tried to cook under pressure. The fear is real. I also hear about it a lot from others. They have the Instant Pot or another brand of electric pressure cooker, but they are afraid to start, never mind knowing where.

Then I started to read other people's recipes and would get angry for other reasons. No wonder people were complaining all the time about cooking in the Instant Pot! Nobody taught them the science! Nobody taught them how! As a result, the internet is full of mostly-rubbish, bland recipes because people were never taught the science and how to convert a stovetop recipe for an electric pressure cooker. You cannot simply follow stovetop recipes without modification.

So why the Instant Pot, or electric pressure cookers in general? I often like to say to people, "Do you want butter chicken with only 10 minutes of work?" Their eyes light up! "Well," I continue, "you can do that and so much more!"

With the Instant Pot, if you are disabled and have mobility issues, you don't have to stand in the kitchen while cooking; if you are neurodivergent, there aren't a lot of things vying for your attention. When cooking under pressure, you just set it and walk away. I have all sorts of tips and tricks to save on kitchen and food prep pain. If you work, you can have wonderfully delicious and complex foods without the fuss and time.

I cook at least 90 percent of my meals in the Instant Pot. I started with the Duo Plus six-quart (5.68 L) and a month later bought the three-quart (2.84 L). This is so I can cook larger quantities of meals with sauce in the six-quart while preparing the rice in the three-quart. Both are also used to make dog food. I have a dog who is allergic to all store-bought food and treats, so we must make everything for our dogs from scratch.

Then I got the Instant Pot Max. Then the eight-quart (7.57 L) Instant Pot Duo Crisp + Air Fryer combo. Then I got another six-quart (5.68 L) Duo. And then I got a Ninja Foodi Deluxe. If I had to choose one to recommend for most disabled people's use, it would be either the Instant Pot Max, if you want to jar food but don't plan to do it in large batches, or an eight-quart Ninja Foodi Deluxe, as it is the best pressure cooker–air fryer combo. Note that the weight of the Ninja Foodi Deluxe may be prohibitive if you have mobility issues.

Then I branched off and started using the Instant Vortex Pro air fryer. And then I got other brands of air fryer ovens to try. If I had room for more electric pressure cookers and air fryers, I would get more.

Not only are they helpful for those with mobility issues and pain disorders, but electric pressure cookers are great if you have certain conditions that make eating food difficult. If you need soft meals, they beat a slow cooker because meals take less time to cook with better results. They are also perfect for neurodivergent people, especially when executive function is affected.

If we add another intersection of marginalization, things become even more complicated. When able-bodied, it can be difficult enough—if not impossible—to find culturally appropriate foods if you are not from a white western European background, especially if you live outside of a major metropolitan area. Also, a lot of Indigenous and non–western European cultural foods have been colonized and whitewashed, or outright erased.

When you add disability on top of the whitewashing of food, access to culturally appropriate foods is impossible unless you know a person who knows a person who can get it and deliver it to you.

I personally grew up immersed in a variety of cultures. My natal heritage is 50 percent British and 50 percent eastern European, second generation on both sides. I grew up in neighbourhoods heavily populated by new Canadians who fled partition, political persecution, and war. When I was a teen, I was adopted into a Panjabi Sikh family. Food was very much a part of the cultures of my upbringing. While I had access to many culturally appropriate foods, there were parts of my own culture that I could not access. I grew up being both the colonizer and the colonized.

As I was writing this book, I thought a lot about my friend Roopa. She gave me permission to share part of her story. Her parents are Panjabi Sikhs. She grew up in a very white part of southern Ontario. Outside of her immediate family, she was often the only South Asian person in her life.

To survive whiteness and to gain a sense of belonging among her peers, she rejected the foods of her home. As she got older, other traumas compounded her fraught relationship with food, especially the foods of her culture. It wasn't until she reached her late 30s that she began to explore this more, beginning to work through the traumas and cultural erasure inflicted upon her because of whiteness and colonization. The process toward a diagnosis of ADHD added more complexity to her story.

And I, as a white person, along with many other white people, have had unfettered, trauma-free, often colonized and whitewashed access to these foods without a second thought to the violence behind this access. Roopa's story, and all the stories of the people I grew up with who share that experience, gave me a lot of pause and direction in my work around food, culture, and accessibility. The loss I felt when I could no longer cook is a fraction of the loss experienced by people of colour, especially Indigenous people whose food culture was criminalized.

It is essential to survival that people have access to culturally appropriate foods. Mental and physical health depend on this. As a white person, I passionately believe that I have a necessary role to play in the decolonization of food. I've developed recipes from a variety of cultural backgrounds that teach the necessary skills for people of all backgrounds to not only source a lot of what they need to cook but also prepare food in a way that is as true to the original cuisine as possible.

Every time someone asks me "Why the Instant Pot?" I give them the above gist and then say, "I could write you a book explaining it all and give you recipes as a jumping-off point. By the time I'm done with you, you'll have all the tools you need to create your own recipe book and figure out how to make your kitchen work for you instead of you working in the kitchen."

The kitchen is the worst room in the house if you are disabled. I'm about to change that and make life easier for everyone.

Well, here you have it. Let your adventures begin!

COMMON SYMPTOMS OF DIFFERENT DISABILITIES AND HOW THIS BOOK WILL HELP

Many disabilities share symptoms. If you have mobility issues and/or a pain disorder, if you have an autoimmune disorder, or if you have ADHD or are autistic, these shared symptoms may include:

- Pain
- Fatigue
- Impaired executive function, a.k.a. brain fog
- Insomnia
- Wildly fluctuating "spoon levels" that make planning ahead difficult
- Chronic illness

And of course, all these things can affect our mood, especially our motivation.

You might be unfamiliar with the spoon theory and talking about energy in terms of "spoons." Spoons are used as a metaphor to help visualize how much stored energy you have. It's important to know this because if you use all your "spoons" in one day, the consequence could be days in bed. Most people have entire cups of energy that they can spend during a day. They need to do very little to replenish those cups. Those of us with disabilities that result in chronic fatigue have a few spoonfuls of energy on any given day, if we are lucky. And it requires much more self-care to replenish that energy.

This cookbook is designed to first help you get your kitchen in order. It's also designed to make sure you don't lose focus or get overwhelmed when organizing, planning, prepping, cooking, and storing meals. But most importantly, it isn't prescriptive and allows for a lot of room to change things for your specific needs.

Taking steps to prevent fatigue and store up "spoons" instead of always overspending is important, even before you start organizing, planning, prepping,

cooking, and storing. We don't talk enough about respecting our body cues and how we can be productive without ableism getting in the way. This is thanks to the internalized ableism that can sound like "Stop being lazy. Just push through it. You aren't trying hard enough!"

I have developed a way to plan my day that is based in mindfulness, as well as respecting and appreciating my disabilities instead of looking at them as something to overcome. I don't do anything in this cookbook until I have assessed what my body is telling me. I assess this at least twice a day.

When it's the beginning of my working hours, I check in with my body and assess how many "spoons" I have on a scale of 1 to 10. Then I look at the spreadsheet I created that lists tasks I can do based on that number. During lunch, I reassess to see if my "spoons" are higher or lower than the initial number and adjust my daily tasks accordingly. Some days, tasks need to be removed. Other days, tasks get added. By the end of the day, I feel good about the things I've accomplished, I feel great mentally, and my pain levels are still manageable instead of screaming at me.

Here is the table with my tasks. I started it at 10 "spoons" for some good cognitive behavioural positive reinforcement. Of course, your tasks will look different because our lives are different. Use my table as a jumping-off point to give you an outline of what your spreadsheet will look like. It's important to note that it will take some time to get it just right for your situation. I had to adjust mine a few times as I overestimated or underestimated how many "spoons" would be spent on some tasks. This is okay! The whole point is to create something that ends up working for your needs, that respects and appreciates your unique brand of disability.

10 SPOONS: PICK 4 ACTIVITIES	9 SPOONS: PICK 4 ACTIVITIES	8 SPOONS: PICK 4 ACTIVITIES	7 SPOONS: PICK 3 ACTIVITIES	6 SPOONS: PICK 3 ACTIVITIES
Write 2,000 words (counts as 2 activities)	Write 1,800 words (counts as 2 activities)	Write 1,600 words (counts as 2 activities)	Write 1,400 words (counts as 2 activities)	Write 1,200 words (counts as 2 activities)
Cook	Cook	Cook	Cook	Cook
Photography study	Photography study	Photography study	Photography study	Photography study
Photography	Photography	Photography	Photography	Photography
Develop ideas	Develop ideas	Develop ideas	Develop ideas	Develop ideas
Recipe study	Recipe study	Recipe study	Recipe study	Recipe study
Update Patreon and/or website	Update Patreon and/or website	Update Patreon and/or website	Update Patreon and/or website	Update Patreon and/or website
Website maintenance if needed	Website maintenance if needed	Website maintenance if needed	Website maintenance if needed	Website maintenance if needed
Update Instagram	Update Instagram	Update Instagram	Update Instagram	Update Instagram
Edit cookbook	Edit cookbook	Edit cookbook	Edit cookbook	Edit cookbook

5 SPOONS: PICK 2 ACTIVITIES	4 SPOONS: PICK 2 ACTIVITIES	3 SPOONS: PICK 2 ACTIVITIES	2 SPOONS: PICK 1 ACTIVITY	1 SPOON: PICK 1 ACTIVITY
Write 1,000 words	Write 800 words	Write 600 words	Write 400 words	Write 200 words
Cook	Cook	Cook side dish	Cook side dish	Cook side dish
Photography study	Photography study	Photography study	Photography study	Photography study
Photography	Photography	Photography	Develop ideas	Develop ideas
Develop ideas	Develop ideas	Develop ideas	Recipe study	Recipe study
Recipe study	Recipe study	Recipe study	Update Instagram	Update Instagram
Update Patreon and/ or website	Update Patreon and/ or website	Update Instagram	Edit cookbook	Edit cookbook
Website maintenance if needed	Website maintenance if needed	Edit cookbook		
Update Instagram	Update Instagram			
Edit cookbook	Edit cookbook			

MUST-HAVE ITEMS TO
CRIP UP YOUR KITCHEN

It's not easy to create a disability-friendly kitchen. And it's not cheap. Ableism rules the world. If we look for products to make our disabled lives better and easier, the messaging we receive is not good. Because of this, we can be hesitant to share our disability tips. As a result, a lot of what we find on the internet is written by the abled, and it is worthless because of inherent ableism.

So, here are 15 essential and tested items for a disability-friendly kitchen. The items are to help solve mobility issues and to reduce pain while in the kitchen. I bought every single item on this list. It costs quite a bit of money to make your kitchen disability friendly. Even so, this list was created with budget in mind. If you can't afford these items, consider putting them on your wish list.

Electric pressure cooker—six quarts (5.68 L) minimum ($100–$150). An electric pressure cooker really is a must-have if you are disabled. I prefer the Instant Pot brand because it has the best built-in safety features, weighs the least, and is the most cost efficient. It will become the thing that anchors your disability-friendly kitchen. I wouldn't have started this cookbook talking about it if I didn't believe that with every fibre of my being. If I had to choose a six-quart model that would work for the most people, it would be the Instant Pot Max because it doubles as a pressure canner.

Bread machine ($100–$150). I don't know where I would be without my bread machine. While not cheap, they are not overly expensive either. I save so much on my grocery bill and cut a lot of food waste. Quickly it pays for itself. We do not eat enough bread to buy loaves at the store. I can easily make fresh pizza dough or roti without having to use my hands to knead. Just dump ingredients and walk away.

A masala dabba or three ($25–$50). Even if you don't do a lot of Indian cooking, the masala dabba is a handy spice and herb storage container. It cuts down movements around the kitchen as you gather all your herbs and spices. And they take up less space than most spice racks. You can have a minimum of seven spices in one handy-dandy place.

The lid seals tight to keep everything fresh. I can't open it without using a butter knife to pry the lid off. But that extra step is totally worth it to avoid pain levels rising while gathering everything I need to cook. And it saves a lot of space in my cramped kitchen.

A decent chef's knife ($40–$60). I cannot stress this one enough. I get angry every time I think about how much money I wasted on other items, such as mandoline slicers that I couldn't use because of the grasping issue. You don't have to spend much on one. They slice without needing much pressure. You don't need to buy a block of knives. Start your knife collection one at a time.

Immersion blender with attachments ($30–$140). An immersion blender with attachments is essential to a disability-friendly kitchen, especially if you have a kitchen that lacks counter space. This saves you from having to chop onions, and you can use the immersion blender when making my Butter Chicken (page 72) or other things that need to be puréed.

Three-in-one peeler, corer, slicer ($23–$35). You don't need gimmicky items to enjoy peeled, cored, and sliced apples and pears, curly fries, or a variety of other fruits and vegetables that you need specially prepared because of chewing issues or your desire to dehydrate them. Even though you hand-turn these devices, it's better than having to push on something. Pushing motions lead to worsening tendon issues and aggravate certain types of arthritis. Even with the loss of full function of my thumbs, I am still able to easily use this device.

A good garlic press ($20–$40). Once, I was the fool who bought a cheap garlic press from Walmart. It required a lot of pressure to press the garlic. So much pressure that a handle broke off while I was trying to press some garlic—my mobility issues are not related to strength. You don't have to spend a lot for a good garlic press.

Jar opener ($15–$20). It took me a while to find a jar opener that works for my mix of hand-related mobility issues. The worst type for me was the kind that has an edge with teeth. The type that does work for me is a rubber easy-grip variety with holes for four different jar lid sizes.

Counter chair/step stool ($100–$150). Having a counter chair and step stool has been a pain saver for sure. I'm a very short dude, and counter heights are too tall for me to mix and stir, chop, etc. in a way that is ergonomic and doesn't result in a lot of pain. Counters are also too tall for me to access when I am using my wheelchair.

A counter chair not only makes me the right height for counters but also allows me to sit while prepping food. The built-in step stool is a bonus: I don't have to drag a chair around to get things from shelves higher than the bottom one. And I don't need to stand on counters.

oxo Good Grips stainless steel locking tongs or similar ($15–$20). If you have grasping issues like I do, you have a tough time finding good tongs. I wish I had been told about oxo Good Grips tongs years ago. Not only are they amazingly comfortable, but you don't need to use a lot of pressure to grasp things with the tongs, and they spring back easily.

Cutting boards that have a handle and non-slip feet ($25–$50). Again, if you're like me and have issues with your hands, you need cutting boards that not only are easy to move around but also won't slip while preparing food. Just buy all the oxo Good Grips items,

including cutting boards. You can't go wrong. This is another thing I wish I had learned about earlier. It's unbelievable how much non-slip cutting boards with a handle relieve pain and help with a variety of mobility issues.

Compression arthritis gloves ($13–$25). Compression arthritis gloves are yet another thing I wish I had learned about decades ago. Not even my rheumatologist recommended them. I became aware of them only because I saw them in a cooking video on YouTube. I wear mine almost all the time. Yes, even when cooking. I just put latex-free exam gloves overtop of them when I'm in the kitchen.

Spice and nut grinder ($40–$60). The reason I'm including a spice and nut grinder is that it helps to cut down on your grocery bill. Instead of buying ground cinnamon, ground cumin, ground cloves, etc., buy large containers of these items as whole spices and grind them yourself. Also, freshly ground spices have much better flavour. Ignore ableist messaging that comes with those who swear a mortar and pestle is the only way.

Multi egg slicer ($20–$30). A multi egg slicer is good for more than slicing eggs. You can use it to slice a variety of soft produce, such as strawberries, white mushrooms, and grapes. The less chopping and dicing you need to do by hand, the more enjoyment you will get while cooking because you are cutting back on physical pain and reserving "spoons."

Pasta roller or French rolling pin ($50–$100). Get rid of your rolling pin with handles. Instead, get a pasta roller—either a hand-crank one or one that attaches to your stand mixer—to roll things such as pie crusts, flatbreads, and crackers. Your pies will be smaller, but the "spoons" saved is a great trade-off. If you can't afford a pasta roller, get a French rolling pin. French rolling pins have tapered ends, making use of the laws of physics in terms of force distribution. Very little pressure is needed when rolling. This makes it easier to roll those circular items, as the force is evenly distributed.

IF YOU COULD HAVE IT ALL— OR AT LEAST MOST OF IT

If money were not an issue, we would all have designer kitchens with low counters and prep spaces with every single spot optimized for our specific disabilities. Then we could perhaps understand this idea of the kitchen being the heart of the home. We would also have every appliance and tool we could dream of, including those cute retro ones. If we could have it all.

That is the dream scenario.

If you were given a bunch of gift cards and could create your dream shopping wish list, what would it look like? I have 12 items I think you should have on that list. These are all items I was fortunate enough to accumulate over the years.

High-speed blender ($50–$150). If you don't already have one, a blender is the first thing you should buy after you have all your must-have kitchen tools. It doesn't need to be anything fancy. I use mine mainly for making masalas and hummus (page 56). Sometimes I will use it to blend a can of diced tomatoes, but that is rare since my immersion blender can do that job.

More than one electric pressure cooker ($100–$380). I have six! That is not a typo. They are a mix of Instant Pot and Ninja brand multi-purpose pressure cookers. I have one three-quart (2.84 L), three six-quarts (5.68 L), and two eight-quarts (7.57 L). If I had room, I would have more. The newest addition to my kitchen, the eight-quart Ninja Foodi Deluxe XL, with TenderCrisp technology, also works as a food dehydrator. There are no words to describe what it's like to have the ability to cook two weeks of food at one go, or to no longer have to put aside days I want to cook, if it's also a dog food–making day.

A food dehydrator ($100–$250). I love my food dehydrator. I originally bought it to make homemade "pupperoni" for my dogs. It has also come in handy to dehydrate herbs such as my catnip—I freeze most of my herbs—and fruits such as apples, pears, and chili peppers.

A good chef's knife and santoku knife ($50–$100). It's time to upgrade your knife collection while adding a new one. You can spend a bit of time shopping brands. If you can afford only one more knife, instead of an upgrade and a new knife, then get yourself a decent santoku knife. It makes meal prep easier not only because it slices meat like butter but also because foods don't stick to it.

Good dry-food storage containers ($40–$100). Having good cannisters is not enough. You want good dry-food storage containers, ones that create an airtight seal. A brand I swear by is Komax Biokips. I have a couple of 35-cup (8.3 L) containers I use as breadboxes. I have the butter dish. I have the pasta storage containers. I have the flour and sugar containers. I have a pack that came with multiple sizes for a variety of dry goods. They not only keep foods fresher for longer but also make meal prep easier when I'm grabbing things from my pantry.

Stovetop pressure canner ($250–$300). Why buy a stovetop pressure canner? The short answer is: 46 home-cooked, ready-to-serve meals in your pantry. The long answer can be found in "Food Storage for Less Waste" (page 28) and "Canning or Freezing—Which Is More Disability Friendly?" (page 29).

Vacuum sealer ($100–$400). Freezing food is an easy storage solution. You are probably storing leftovers in clunky containers in your fridge. A vacuum sealer not only helps to increase storage space in your fridge and freezer but also makes food last up to five times longer.

Electric can opener ($40–$50). If you have arthritis, tendinitis, or neuropathic pain in general, eventually you are going to go through every type of manual or robotic can opener, wasting money. Just skip to the end and buy an electric can opener. Not only will you save money in the long run, but immediately you will also save "spoons."

Air fryer lid for the Instant Pot ($100–$150). It's not often that I air fry, but I'm very glad I purchased the Instant Pot Duo Crisp + Air Fryer, instead of just a stand-alone eight-quart (7.57 L), for those times I want to bake things. Great news! You can buy the air fryer lid with some accessories to fit your existing six-quart (5.68 L) or eight-quart Instant Pot. And, as with the Ninja Foodi XL, this will also allow you to use your Instant Pot as a small-batch food dehydrator.

As my disabilities progressed, my ability to safely use the oven diminished. Now, things I once baked in the oven are air fried. There is one downside to this option: it takes a bit longer to air fry things using this method compared with an oven-style air fryer.

Oven-style air fryer ($150–$300). The oven-style Instant Vortex Pro and Crownful 19-Quart (18 L) Air Fryer Toaster Oven are amazing air fryers. They each have two types of rotisserie options, multiple cooking racks, and a large capacity. Plus, they cook foods super fast, much faster than basket-style air fryers. They also work as dehydrators. They are basically tiny convection ovens at a reasonable price. If you buy either an oven-style air fryer or electric pressure cooker–air fryer combo, buy a multi-tier dehydrator rack that will fit across devices.

Food processor with dicing disc ($120–$300). While being able to chop things with an immersion blender attachment is nice, it is limiting. You can chop only a couple of cups at a time. You can't grate anything. And you can't dice anything. You want a food processor with dicing ability. The best one on the market is from KitchenAid; it's also the most expensive, but it's oh so worth it.

Stand mixer with food processor attachment ($200–$650). The crème de la crème. If dreams were reality. Some brands cost more than a stove. Why are they so expensive? Because they are worth every single nickel owing to their durability and lifespan. Amazon has sales on stand mixers all the time. Keep your eyes on Used.ca, Kijiji, or Amazon Warehouse Deals for used ones. Eventually, you may find yourself with all the attachments.

ORGANIZING THE MOST UNFRIENDLY ROOM IN THE HOME—YOUR KITCHEN

When my partner and I first looked at our rental home, we fell in love at once. It was built in the early 1900s. Everything inside was brand new, and everything outside was restored. We even loved our kitchen, small compared with modern kitchens but bigger than the kitchen from which we were moving.

Our love affair with the kitchen quickly grew to hate. A whole bank of counters is unusable because, instead of the usual two-foot (60 cm) depth, they are one foot (30 cm) deep. There is a beautiful original built-in cabinet with glass doors, butcher-block countertop, and drawers, but the height between the countertop and the shelving with glass doors isn't tall enough to house our microwave, leaving us with about four square feet (0.37 m^2) of usable counter space. We have a huge walk-in pantry—bigger than one of our bathrooms—but it's outside of the kitchen.

Then there are the usual things that make kitchens ableist. The counters are too tall to sit at with a regular chair, or wheelchair, and are too tall for people to work at if they're under five foot six (168 cm), which is me. Not enough cupboards in the work triangle. The space between fridge and counters barely meets the minimum distance requirement, which makes the kitchen hardly manoeuvrable in a wheelchair.

Over the years, I've been able to arrange and rearrange things to make workflow easier in the kitchen. I've also been able to create more usable workspace with minimal cost.

Buy extra workspace, cupboards, and drawers—kitchen carts ($175–$400). This sounds expensive but it isn't. I was able to get a kitchen cart that has lower counters, drawers, cupboards, a tea towel holder, and more, on casters, for a very reasonable price. The layout of our kitchen is such that there is a lot of unusable space. I made that space usable by adding this piece, while also creating much-needed extra storage space.

Eventually, I bought a second, smaller kitchen cart for some more needed storage in my work triangle.

Use a small kitchen table for prep space and countertop storage ($40–$150). If your kitchen has a small nook for an eat-in area, use that nook for your new work triangle including your kitchen carts. This allows you to sit while prepping. On that table, you can also keep an electric pressure cooker or two, so that you can do it all in that one space.

Use shoe racks to create extra vertical countertop storage ($50–$100). You can buy counter organizers, but they cost a premium. You can do the exact same thing with ClosetMaid shoe racks. I have one on my kitchen table that stores two Instant Pots and my vacuum sealer, cutting boards, and masala dabbas. I have another on my built-in counters to store other things.

Keep your most-used spices, small appliances, and cooking utensils within reach. When I sit at my kitchen table to prep and cook, to the left of me on the usually unusable, one-foot-deep counters are my electric can opener, bread machine, and food dehydrator. In front of me are two Instant Pots, my vacuum sealer, a cutting board, and one masala dabba.

To the right of me is the small, just over one-square-foot (0.09 m2) kitchen cart with my most-used sauces and bulk spice containers, more masala dabbas holding my most-used herbs and spices, onions, potatoes, vacuum bags, and my recipe book.

Behind me is the bigger kitchen cart that holds everything else I use most often in the kitchen: Instant Pot accessories, other small appliances, cooking utensils, more cookbooks, canning tools, and more. My kitchen sink is in the peninsula behind my large kitchen cart.

On the regular counters, in what would traditionally be the work triangle, are more electric pressure cookers and my stand mixer.

Over time, after spending about $500 for carts and racks, I was able to create a whole new work triangle. It is completely suited to my disabilities and mobility issues. It is all within reach while I'm using my wheelchair, without my having to manoeuvre around corners that don't have enough space.

It's never going to be ready for a magazine cover. For that, I would need $100,000 at my disposal. But it is functional. And that is the goal.

When it's time to cook, I still need to go into the pantry for canned goods. But thanks to organization, that is a snap.

ORGANIZING THE PANTRY AND MAKING GROCERY LISTS A SNAP

My pantry is organized not only for my mobility issues but also to keep my autistic self happy while keeping my OCD in check, and to help my partner find things and put things away in a way that is friendly for his ADHD. It's also designed to make grocery lists a snap without a surprise "What do you need from the store?" that leaves you stumped.

If you're not fortunate enough to have a walk-in pantry and use cupboards or an IKEA pantry, or a mix of spaces throughout the house, my method will still work for you. Plus, you will always know what you have on hand and where it can be found. Even better, you can easily change this method to fit your needs.

Install the Pantrify app by Gartorware—desktop and mobile. I went through a minimum of 20 different apps before finding one that is hands down the best. You can access Pantrify via a browser, which allows you to turn it into a desktop app. You can also install it on your phone or tablet (it's found on both Google Play and the App Store).

Pantrify allows for multiple users via quick invite using your Google account. It automatically syncs across all users and devices. It has a bar code scanner. You can add images. You can easily create shopping lists in the app based on criteria you set. You can divide up multiple rooms in the house and keep track of inventory of whatever you want.

I have created one room called "Food." In that room are multiple areas: my partner's area, the pantry, the freezer, home-canned goods, and the kitchen, which includes the fridge. Whenever something comes in the house, it gets scanned into the app. As we use things, they are removed from the app.

Organize your pantry into smaller groupings. If I had my way, I would have things organized by grocery store aisle. But I live with someone who has ADHD. That wouldn't work for them when it comes time to put away the groceries or find things when I ask for help. As a happy middle ground, I have organized the pantry into smaller groupings.

One grouping has dog food–making items. Another, tomato products and canned beans. Another, international food items. Another, coffee beans. Another, baking needs in clearly labelled airtight containers. Another, home-canned goods.

I take pictures of everything and their locations and add those images to the Pantrify app to help my partner find things and put them away. Especially the home-canned goods.

When I need to shop the pantry, I grab a reusable

shopping bag and just put everything in it, or I put a basket on my lap when using my wheelchair.

Everything else is in my work triangle.

Put a shopping list and pen on the fridge door. As soon as we're low on an item in the fridge or in my work triangle, we write it on the paper grocery list attached to the fridge door. We also add things as they're running low in the pantry. This is because I grab the grocery list once a week to shop online, and I like to mark things as placed in my cart as I shop. The grocery list we use is organized by area. You can find it in the appendix.

If paper lists aren't your thing, this is where, once again, Pantrify comes in. Shopping lists can be created with a tap based on conditions you set up when adding a product for the first time, or they can be added manually.

We use a mix of both the app and paper for two reasons:

1. If my partner forgets to write something on the paper list, the app is there as a backup and vice versa, leaving little room for error and the brain fart that happens when someone asks "What do you need from the store?" moments before they plan to walk out the door.

2. I can easily see what's on hand when I'm doing meal planning or want to cook to bust anxiety.

All three of the above tools and methods can easily be changed to fit your household. Happy organizing!

HOW TO MEAL PLAN

If you're like me, you can't count the number of times you've read a "How to Meal Plan" blog post and thought, "They want me to do what?! Hello, wasted food!" For me, a lot of food waste used to come from planning daily meals that required daily cooking and never having enough "spoons" to cook and eat everything I bought. Even meal kits like HelloFresh resulted in an enormous amount of food waste because cooking those meals, even with adaptations, would wipe me out for days.

The way I meal plan can be easily adapted to fit your unique situation. It allows for a huge amount of flexibility with little to no food waste, all while eating healthy—*healthy* meaning good sources of nutrients, not some diet culture thing.

Pick a minimum of nine recipes you love and figure out the staple items. I don't know many people—

abled or disabled—who regularly eat as wide a variety of food as I do. Most people I know tend to eat the same basic types of meals that include some type of meat, some type of veg, and some type of starch, all within the same cuisine type. If they eat anything outside of that, it tends to be takeout or delivery. In my opinion, it makes for incredibly boring meals.

I like a lot of variety in my food; much of what I eat is Asian and Mediterranean food but from different regions, which makes for diverse flavour profiles. Also, I have a *lot* of dietary restrictions and needs because of food allergies, a body that doesn't like to keep good ferritin or iron stores, irritable bowel syndrome (IBS), and reactive hypoglycemia. I pick meals based not on calorie counts but on ingredients that don't trigger my form of IBS and are rich in vitamins and minerals. I choose foods that are lower in carbs and high in protein and fat to lessen my overproduction of insulin, which happens when I eat carbs, as well as foods that are good sources of iron so I can eat more than the daily recommended amount without having to take a supplement my body doesn't like to absorb.

Finding food that meets all my restrictions and needs would be exceedingly difficult if I did not have staple go-to foods. Also, mealtimes would be boring as heck.

Picking a minimum of nine staple recipes not only makes managing the above easier but also takes the guesswork out of grocery shopping, allows me to shop less frequently, makes food prep days quick and efficient with little to no preplanning, and reduces the time required for cooking and meal planning.

When it's time to cook, I make most of my staple items in double batches so that I have a minimum of six meals precooked instead of three or four. If you do the math, that's a minimum of 54 meals planned a month in advance, or just under one month of lunches and suppers.

The exceptions for double batches are recipes that fill the electric pressure cooker to its maximum precooked capacity, like my Doukhobor Borshch (page 205) and Effin' Good Chili (page 95).

Instead of doing meal planning a week at a time, plan a couple of weeks or a month ahead. This tip works with the preceding tip and the next tip. Simply put, it makes everything about meal planning, prepping, and cooking easier while significantly reducing the number of "spoons" required. Also, it reduces how often you need to shop while still leaving room to cook things spontaneously when you crave a certain something that is not a staple.

It also reduces food waste, which saves a heck of a lot of money. Say goodbye to having things sit in the fridge until they go bad because you either don't feel like that thing anymore or simply didn't have the "spoons" to cook that week.

I've provided an example of a meal planner sheet in the appendix. Once every other week, I sit down and add dog food–making days. Then I plan batch cooking days around those. In the beginning, I plan around making my nine staple meals so I can fully stock my

pantry with canned goods and my freezer with vacuum-sealed portions. My planning is flexible so that I can move things around as needed and always have meals on hand.

In short order, far fewer days are spent meal planning, and, thanks to the next tip, I have weeks of meals in my pantry.

If you have the "spoons," spend a few days in a row cooking a lot of food, and then don't cook for weeks. I cook only a few times a month. My pantry almost always has a minimum of three weeks' worth of pressure-canned, home-cooked meals. I'll have some months when my pre-existing health conditions are nice enough to let me cook every day for a week, and then I don't have to cook for a couple of months. In those couple of months, my freezers get filled with things from "How to Meal Prep" (page 20), which keeps my pantry full of nutritious meals that meet all my complex dietary restrictions and needs.

This also comes in handy when my immune system condition is trying to take me down because there is always something to eat and I can just concentrate on rest and dealing with medical issues.

Once you've stocked up your cupboards and freezer with precooked meals, restock when you're down to two meals of something. This tip works in concert with the previous tips and those in the next chapter. Once you get to this tip, your pantry and/or cupboards will be full of at least a month's worth of meals after cooking nine times. After this time, you'll be down to cooking only a couple of times a month when it's time to replenish a food item. If you can't manage that because a chronic health condition is really kicking your arse, then it truly is okay to buy prepared foods without guilt—if you can find things that meet dietary requirements.

The point of all of this is to make mealtimes and cooking vastly easier to help reduce the number of "spoons" exhausted. This will also help reduce flare-ups because you have more "spoons" for self-care.

HOW TO MEAL PREP

Meal prep can take so much time, especially if you are disabled. Wouldn't it be nice if meal prep were easier? I often find myself reading recipes that say "10 minutes' prep time," and the reality ends up being at least three times that amount because of my mobility issues. Then, when it comes time to make the recipe, it's just too many steps hidden in overly concise instructions.

You may have already read some meal prep tips and tricks. Every piece of meal prep advice I've ever read has been written by an abled person with the assumption that someone is going to cook every night of the week, telling you to prep things and then stick it in the fridge. Yeah, no thanks. You're just asking that I throw everything in the compost after two weeks.

The following is how I meal prep. As with how I meal plan, my method can be easily adapted to your unique needs.

Spend time every two weeks prechopping and freezing often-used ingredients. This is how I do it. Adapt my process so that it works for your form of disability. I do it this way because I can't stand for more than a couple of minutes because of the benign tumour on my spinal cord in my lower back and mechanical issues with my feet.

You will need a few items for this:

- A cutting board
- A good sharp knife (will be used minimally)
- A blender
- A food processor or the chopper attachment on your immersion blender
- Food storage containers or a vacuum sealer and bags
- Freezer labels
- Freezer bags or a vacuum sealer and bags
- A kitchen counter chair
- A memory foam floor mat or yoga mat

Every other Friday or Saturday—those are just the days that work best for me—I grab my Surface Pro and headphones and go into the kitchen. I plug myself in to music and put what I've determined are my staple items on my prep table: a whole bunch of bell peppers, onions, cilantro, serrano peppers, garlic, and ginger. If you don't have a lot of prep space or a place to put a working table, use your stovetop. Just make sure the stove is turned off. If you use a wheelchair all the time, then you probably already have a table set up for prep.

I grab my compost bin and the above needed items.

I sit down and prep away.

I cut one onion into eight pieces, stick it in the chopper of my immersion blender or food processor, chop, stick it in a storage container, and label it. I repeat until I've chopped an entire bag of onions (approximately eight to ten onions). I buy medium-sized yellow onions in a bag, since one medium-sized yellow onion equals about one cup (250 mL) of chopped onions.

So that's eight to ten recipes' worth of onions done in about 15 minutes. I put these small containers in my fridge freezer, ready to pull out when it's time to cook something. A wonderful thing about cooking in an electric pressure cooker is that you don't need to defrost anything before cooking.

Next, I go through my bell peppers. I have some recipes that call for a whole green bell pepper, some that call for a whole red bell pepper, some that call for a mix of orange and red peppers, etc. When I see that I'm getting low on peppers, I buy four green bell peppers, four red bell peppers, and two bags of mixed orange and red bell peppers.

I sit and seed my green peppers. Cut them in big chunks. Stick them in the chopper attachment for my immersion blender. Chop. Vacuum seal. (If you don't have a vacuum sealer, use freezer bags. I recommend freezer bags instead of storage containers for bell peppers because you can press all the air out, which helps to retain the flavour and prevent freezer burn.) I repeat with my red peppers. And I repeat again with my mixed bell peppers, but I slice these in thick pieces, storing them all in recipe-quantity servings.

So that's 12 recipes' worth of bell peppers done in about 20 minutes. These get stored in my deep freezer because of limited space in my fridge freezer.

Next, I chop up cilantro and put it in half-cup (125 mL) storage containers, since that's a common quantity for my recipes that call for cilantro. This takes only a couple of minutes, and it gets stored in my fridge freezer.

Finally, I make a bunch of Ginger-Garlic Masala (page 44) and Herb Butter (page 50), stick it in half-cup (125 mL) containers, and put it in my fridge freezer. I also make some Ginger-Garlic Masala without the serrano peppers for those of my recipes that call for minced ginger and garlic without the added heat of the chili pepper.

Once a month, I also shred a cabbage, divide it into five-cup (1.25 L) quantities for my Doukhobor Borshch (page 205), and freeze it.

Having these staples and the large ingredients always prepped and waiting in the freezer allows me to use my Instant Pot as a tool to manage anxiety caused by my complex post-traumatic stress syndrome.

In less than one hour, I've prepared most of what I'll need for two weeks' worth of meals. Meat is already frozen in 454-gram (1 lb) portions the day it gets delivered from my grocer, which is usually a Saturday.

One hour is a lot in one sitting. Not only can it drain all your "spoons," but if you have lower back issues, the sitting is going to send your pain through the roof. And if you have issues with your feet, you may not be able to stand, even with the best of shoes and orthotics.

The solution: Don't do it all at once. Do one item, like the onions. Then do something to refill your spent "spoons" and/or relieve pain. Come back. Repeat. This is also where the floor mat comes in. You can stop at any time, lie on the floor, and do whatever light stretches you need to do to relieve pain.

If financially feasible, purchase already peeled, minced, and cut food items. While I have many recipes where I replace minced garlic and ginger with my Ginger-Garlic Masala, it's not possible with all the recipes I've created because some call for one or the other. Minced ginger is far outside of my budget with the amount of ginger I go through in a month. However, I recently discovered that where I live, peeled garlic cloves are cheaper per 100 grams than whole garlic. For once, a disability-friendly peeled item that is cheaper!

The same goes for chopped veggies, prepeeled oranges, etc., *if* financially workable. Where already chopped fresh veggies are way too expensive, go with frozen chopped veggie mixes and frozen veggies in general. Frozen vegetables have more nutrients than fresh. It's true. Frozen vegetables are flash-frozen right after being picked, which locks in nutrients, whereas fresh vegetables lose their nutrients as they sit because they're in a continuous dying process as soon as they're picked. Don't let diet culture shame you for using frozen produce.

Buying these things has a significant impact on making meal prep easier and manageable for those of us who are disabled.

Cook hard-boiled eggs in your Instant Pot. I don't eat hard-boiled eggs because I have an anaphylactic reaction to egg whites. But both my dogs have severe food and environmental allergies, so we must cook everything they eat. Their main meals include eggs as a source of protein.

Before my partner took over cooking for the dogs, I was having a heck of a time with the egg part. It would take me 30 minutes to peel all the hard-boiled eggs required for one week of food. I had searched for how to cook hard-boiled eggs to make them easy to peel, and abled people said the Instant Pot method doesn't work. But someone I know who is also disabled gave me the following instructions: "Put the eggs on the trivet, add 1 cup [250 mL] water, and do 6 eggs at 5 minutes, 12 at 4, and 18 at 3 minutes. A 6 qt [5.68 L] Instant Pot can hard boil up to 18 eggs."

The result: time to peel eggs is cut down to not even 10 seconds per egg.

But there's a second part to this that I figured out, to make it super easy:

Scissors!

Immediately after the pressure naturally releases, put the eggs in cold water and let them sit for however long you want. Once they're cold, get a pair of kitchen scissors that have that serrated part between the handles. Place the middle of the egg in the serrated part of the scissors. Crack the egg. Pull off the top and bottom of the eggshell. Done! An egg topper will not do the trick. The egg needs to be cracked around the middle.

Always double recipes that call for half of something. Whether that half is half an onion, half a pepper, or one cup (250 mL) of coconut milk (which is roughly half a can), just double the recipe and cook twice as much. Not only does this mean more precooked meals, resulting in more flexible meal planning, but it makes food prep easier because you don't have to prechop ingredients in multiple quantities. You never have to think about what you're pulling out of the freezer or worry about writing and checking quantity on a freezer label.

The same goes if a recipe calls for one and a half pounds of whatever meat. Just pull out three 454-gram (1 lb) portions of whatever frozen meat, and double the rest of the ingredients. Done.

Herbs and spices are the exception for this rule. We are talking about big main ingredients.

HOW TO COOK SAFELY WHEN DISABLED

If you are disabled, there are some basic safety guidelines you should follow in the kitchen. You are probably already familiar with some of them. Others go against everything society tells us about pushing through pain or "overcoming" disability. Disability is not something to overcome. It is something to acknowledge and respect. Without that acknowledgement and respect, you may end up making your disability worse while also setting yourself up to get hurt. Over the years, I have learned

some basic skills that have kept me safe while in the kitchen.

Wear shoes or slippers. Even if you use a wheelchair, make sure your feet are protected. I cannot count how many times I have nearly skewered myself in the foot when dropping a knife. Dropping utensils is difficult to avoid even if one is abled. This guideline is for every kitchen, disabled or not.

Don't reach across an electric pressure cooker/ multicooker. It's weird that I even have to say this—not so much to you, but I must constantly remind myself of this tip. The number of scars I have on the insides of my lower arms from hot inner pot burns!

The funny thing is I would never think of reaching across a pot on the stove. But because the outside walls of the multicooker stay cool, it lures my brain into a false sense of safety. Don't be me. Figure out a way to make your brain think of this appliance the same way it does a pot on a hot stove.

Respect your limitations. You may be really tempted to push through whatever limitations your disability or disabilities pose. After all, the messaging society gives us is very clear here: you are lazy if you don't push through. I am here to tell you that is bullshit. Everyone has limitations. Abled or disabled. Pushing through is a major contributor to injury and depletion of a week's worth of "spoons."

If you start to feel sore while in the kitchen, take a break. Do some stretching. Lie down. Pacing is key. A thing I do is assess my "spoons" in the morning at around ten o'clock and again in the afternoon at around two. I have a chart of activities I'm able to do depending on "spoon" levels (page 8–9). I pick things from the chart accordingly, write it down in my planner, and give myself a sticker when I've completed it. If I do anything else, I also write that down and give myself bonus stickers. After some time, you become very in tune with your body, fatigue, and pain. And injuries decrease.

This also applies to people who are neurodivergent. If you're having a day in which everything is escaping your attention, listen to that. Follow the steps in "How to Meal Prep" (page 20) to create a distraction-free environment in the kitchen.

Sit down to prep if possible. This tip is mainly for people with a variety of mobility issues. If you are not a wheelchair user, it's important to find a good counter chair, which helps you to prep and cook in a good ergonomic position. This lessens fatigue and pain, which results in being less accident prone. If you have a table you can work at, that is better, and a regular chair will do fine.

If you're a wheelchair user, it's best to have a low table at which to prep. If you can find an even lower bench to put small appliances on while you prep and cook, all the better. Put your multicooker, hot plate, etc. down lower than low table height. This allows you to see into the pot and be safer while sautéing. I'm fortunate because my low work table came with bench seating that I use as an extra prep and cooking surface.

Don't cook when low on "spoons." Two of the biggest reasons for injuries in the kitchen are distractions and low energy. To be safe in the kitchen, you need to be as focused as possible. Don't expect full focus. Don't wait until you have full "spoons."

Whether you have brain fog because of physical disability or ADHD sorting issues, or any number of disabilities that cause lapses in focus, your focus is never going to be perfect. That's okay! The trick is to recognize when it's futile to even try.

And no matter what the cause for fatigue is, you could have a lot of great days or be like me, for whom having more than five "spoons" in a day is a rarity. I live at around three "spoons" a day, though it's slowly improving now that I have a wheelchair. I won't cook any main dish if I'm under four "spoons." If I score one to three, then it's side dishes that are dump and cook, or I grab something I already cooked that's in the pantry.

Give you and your disabilities the respect and care they deserve.

USING YOUR ELECTRIC PRESSURE COOKER TO QUASH ANXIETY

You picked your staple recipes. You have them somewhere in physical form, like this cookbook or printed out, if you don't need a screen reader. You always have staple ingredients in the home, ready to go. You are having an anxiety attack at home. Now what? You cook! Why? Cooking is a grounding exercise. Truth.

There is one more thing you need to do before you cook: if possible, put away your electronics. If you can't put away your electronics because you need the screen reader, open your recipe and put your device in distraction-free mode.

Cooking acts as a grounding exercise because it is methodical and forces you to focus on what's immediately in front of you and not on whatever triggered your anxiety.

Make sure your recipe has the required equipment listed. This is important. If you put yourself in a situation where you start thinking about what you need, distractions are going to find their way in, and the anxiety spiral will resume.

Follow the recipe by first gathering your tools and equipment. Then gather your ingredients. Then prep and "mise en place" (organize in advance) your ingredients. Then follow the instructions. Depending on the recipe, you will spend at least 20 minutes grounding and focusing on nothing but what is right in front of you.

You want to do this in your Instant Pot, Ninja Foodi, or equivalent because it doesn't matter if your ingredients are frozen. All you need to do is add a couple more minutes to the time under pressure. There's no need to preplan outside of making sure you always have staple ingredients.

If you have more than one electric pressure cooker or extra inner pots and you are still on edge, repeat until you are good.

Congratulations! Not only did you just do amazing self-care by performing a grounding exercise, but you also did self-care by preparing at least six servings of one meal.

STAPLE PANTRY ITEMS

If you want to use this cookbook as a foundational piece in your disabled kitchen, including as a tool to manage anxiety, here is a list of items you will always want on hand. These ingredients don't cover every recipe, but they do cover the majority and are the most affordable.

HERBS/SPICES

- Sea salt
- Ground cayenne pepper
- Ground black pepper
- Black peppercorns
- Ground turmeric
- Paprika
- Ground cumin
- Cumin seeds
- Cinnamon sticks
- Whole cloves
- Green cardamom pods
- Green cardamom seeds
- Whole black cardamom
- Coriander seeds
- Ground coriander
- Chili powder
- Bay leaves
- Dried oregano
- Dried basil
- Dried thyme
- Fresh basil
- Fresh sage
- Fresh rosemary
- Fresh thyme
- Italian herb seasoning paste (or dry if that's all you can source)
- Cilantro
- Fresh ginger
- Fresh garlic

VEGETABLES

- Jalapeno peppers
- Serrano peppers
- Onions, yellow and red
- Russet potatoes
- Carrots
- Bell peppers, all colours
- Celery
- Frozen mixed vegetables
- Frozen peas

MEAT

- Boneless skinless chicken
- Ground beef

DRY GOODS

- Basmati rice
- Black rice
- Jasmine rice
- Dried red lentils
- Dried black lentils
- Dried chickpeas
- Dried red kidney beans

CANNED GOODS

- Canned red kidney beans
- Canned tomato paste
- Canned diced tomatoes, no salt added
- Canned crushed tomatoes
- Canned tomato sauce
- Canned San Marzano tomatoes
- Canned fire-roasted tomatoes
- Olive oil
- Coconut milk
- Chicken broth

DAIRY

- Full-fat Greek yogourt
- Ghee (clarified butter)

HOW TO CONVERT STOVETOP RECIPES FOR THE ELECTRIC PRESSURE COOKER

The most frequent mistake I see when reading electric pressure cooker recipes, such as Instant Pot recipes, is that they are straight conversions from stovetop/oven to Instant Pot. This results in bland food because the recipes use too large a quantity of liquids. They also use unnecessarily long cook times, including unnecessarily browning meat before cooking.

Science is your friend when it comes to cooking under pressure! Make the science work to your advantage.

You need only one cup (250 mL) of liquids when cooking under pressure. All meat and veg you add to your cooker will add liquid when cooked under pressure. This contributes to the one-cup-of-liquids rule. At a minimum, meat and veg will add half a cup (125 mL) of liquids, so you will need only half a cup of water, unless you are cooking rice, beans, or legumes.

If you're converting a soup recipe, a good rule of thumb is to cut the broth/stock/water amount in half. You can always cut it back more. Better to have a concentrated soup and add water after the pressure has released than to have a flavourless meal.

As an example, in my Doukhobor Borshch recipe (page 205), the liquids are already less than half the stovetop version.

Time under pressure is based on longest cook time of individual ingredients. Until you memorize cook times, an effective way to figure them out is to list all the ingredients. Grab the cook-time chart that came with your electric pressure cooker, look it up online, or use this book. Beside each ingredient, write the time under pressure for that one ingredient. Scan to see what the single longest cook time is. That is the time needed under pressure for your recipe.

Cut items into smaller pieces for less time under pressure. The more surface area per volume an item has, the less time it takes to cook under pressure. As an example, diced potatoes take two minutes while a whole potato takes eight minutes.

Don't waste time browning meat (but sautéing is fine). I wish I could embed videos in physical books so that I could share an amazing one about the Maillard reaction and how it happens when meat is cooked under pressure, negating the need to prebrown meat. The only time meat needs to be somewhat precooked is when a recipe contains ground beef and you want it to be crumbly instead of a giant lump. Also, there are times you will want to sauté aromatics to create different flavour profiles.

Add ingredients from wet to solid. This is to avoid getting the burn warning on your electric pressure cooker. Solid ingredients include viscous items like tomato sauces and paste. If you're doing a dish that calls for a lot of viscous tomato products, add a cup of water before you slowly add the tomato products, and do not stir. If you're making a recipe that calls for ground beef, be sure to deglaze the pot with a quarter cup (60 mL) of water before adding the rest of the ingredients.

If you're in a hurry, preheat liquid-heavy recipes. If you don't want to wait 30 minutes for your liquid-heavy recipes to come to pressure, turn your cooker to Sauté and warm up the ingredients. The warmer the ingredients are to begin with, the faster it will come to pressure.

With few exceptions, 10 minutes of natural release is necessary. Your food begins to cook as it's coming to pressure and continues to cook while pressure is naturally releasing. That's why it takes only four minutes under pressure to cook white rice. If you want to keep your kitchen clean, you also want to let liquid-heavy recipes naturally release fully. Otherwise you will have chunky steam all over your kitchen and your lid caked with junk as things rapidly come to a violent boil when you quick-release pressure.

FOOD STORAGE FOR LESS WASTE

There are three different ways I store food for less waste: dehydration; canning, a.k.a. jarring; and freezing. Each method has its pros and cons. Each method serves a distinct purpose. All of them quickly pay for themselves.

Why you should consider a food dehydrator for food preservation. Pros: I love my food dehydrator. I originally bought it to make homemade "pupperoni" for my dogs. It has also come in handy to dehydrate some herbs like my catnip—I freeze most of my herbs—and to dehydrate fruits such as apples, pears, and chili peppers.

I buy chili peppers in bulk when I don't have enough growing in my AeroGarden. Freezing hot peppers is not good. They lose all their flavour and heat. However, dehydrating them is super easy. You just prepare them— some cut in half with seeds removed, some with just the tops and stems cut off—stick them in the dehydrator before bed, and wake up to preserved chili peppers. Always wear gloves when preparing chili peppers and removing them from the dehydrator.

Then, when it's time to cook with them, you let them soak for a bit in water if serving them as a garnish, chop them dry when adding them to electric pressure cooker recipes, or grind them up to make your own substitutions for things like ground cayenne pepper. Again, remember to always wear gloves when touching them, especially after they've been dehydrated, as the process causes them to sweat capsaicinoids—the stuff that gives chili peppers their heat.

Cons: it takes up a fair amount of space and has a relatively high initial cost.

Why you should consider investing in a vacuum sealer. Pros: This bears repeating. Freezing food is an easy storage solution. You are probably storing leftovers in clunky containers in your fridge. Not only does a vacuum sealer help to increase storage space in your fridge and freezer, but food also lasts up to five times longer when vacuum sealed.

Cons: even the smallest model takes up valuable real estate, and the initial cost can be prohibitive.

Why you should consider canning/jarring. A bit of a warning when it comes to pressure canning: it does take a fair number of "spoons" if you're using a stovetop canner. That said, you will have less food waste if you preserve your food by pressure canning. Also, you don't have to think about pulling anything out of the freezer to defrost. When hungry, you just need to open a jar, reheat, and eat.

The Instant Pot Max does significantly reduce the number of "spoons" required for pressure canning, but you can't jar as much at one time, and it costs twice as much as a stovetop pressure canner. You are limited to four jars. But canning batches of food in two sessions instead of one still requires fewer "spoons." (See the "Canning Steps" chapter on page 32 for instructions on how to pressure can.)

If you don't want to pressure can over multiple sessions, then the next chapter is for you. It also covers the pros and cons more extensively because there are a lot of each.

CANNING OR FREEZING—WHICH IS MORE DISABILITY FRIENDLY?

Several of my recipes can be either canned/jarred or frozen. If you are disabled and considering canning, you may be wondering which method is best for you. The short answer is that it depends.

THE PROS OF FREEZING

Pro of freezing 1: It requires few "spoons." Freezing is an extremely effortless way to preserve food. Because it's so easy, it requires few "spoons" to put food in containers and stick them in the freezer.

Pro of freezing 2: It's cost efficient to begin. There is little in the way of upfront investment for freezing. You will want to buy heavy-duty storage containers that won't need to be replaced as often as storage containers made from thinner plastics. Eventually, you will want a vacuum sealer.

Pro of freezing 3: Food can be stored for an okay amount of time. Depending on the type of food and whether you are freezing in your refrigerator's freezer or a deep freezer, your food can last 2–12 months. This is beneficial because you can cook multiple portions of food at once and freeze them in portion-sized containers that are ready to serve. This saves you from having to cook every day.

THE CONS OF FREEZING

Con of freezing 1: Limited space. If all you have is the freezer in your fridge, then you really can't store much. Having a bigger deep freezer is not necessarily better, which brings me to the next con.

Con of freezing 2: Out of sight, out of mind. The problem I find with freezing precooked, preportioned meals is that I forget what I have frozen as my small deep freezer begins to fill up. I don't have this problem with the meat

I freeze in recipe-sized quantities, as those are always at the top of the freezer and are used fairly quickly.

At least twice a year, I find myself throwing out a lot of frozen meals because they were forgotten about and well beyond their eat-by date. That's a lot of wasted money.

Con of freezing 3: Deep freezers and refrigerator freezers are not disability friendly. Having a deep freezer means a lot of bending over into the freezer to grab things that are near the bottom. If you use a wheelchair, it may simply not be possible. It may also not be possible for a wide range of mobility issues.

The problem is the same for refrigerator freezers. Those that have the freezer on the top can't be reached if you're in a wheelchair. Those that have the freezer on the bottom require bending over or squatting, which poses several problems for people with mobility issues.

The problem with side-by-side refrigerator-freezers is that there's a limited usable zone for people with a variety of mobility issues.

Con of freezing 4: The long-term costs add up. Whether it's because of the forgotten food you have to toss, the fact you need to replace even the best of storage containers, or even the need to buy a deep freezer if you want to store more than a couple of meals, the costs of freezing add up over time.

Con of freezing 5: It requires extra thought for meal planning. Maybe it's just me, but I really don't care for food defrosted in the microwave. You can defrost food in an electric pressure cooker, but it's a bit of a process. Freezing meals means I must always think a day in advance so I can pull a meal out of the freezer and let it safely defrost in my fridge overnight. Often, this means eating meals I'm not really into and wishing I'd taken something else out.

THE PROS OF CANNING

Pro of canning 1: You can store a lot more food. You are limited only by cupboard space and pantry space; cans/jars can be tucked in closets or the laundry room, wherever. There are no restrictions on where you can store your food other than it being a place with little to low light and at room temperature.

Pro of canning 2: Food lasts longer. Food should be eaten within a year of canning, which is quite a long time. You don't have to worry about something getting freezer burned.

Pro of canning 3: You save money in the long term. Canning jars, the screw part of the lids, canning tools, and canners last an exceedingly long time. Years and years. You don't have to replace them nearly as often as you need to replace food storage containers. Replacement lids are not that expensive.

Pro of canning 4: No extra thought for meal planning. Once you are fully stocked with homemade canned goods—which takes only a few weeks of big-batch cooking to achieve—all you need to do when hungry is to go to wherever your jars are stored and decide. The worst thing that can happen is you get option paralysis.

Pro of canning 5: Little to no food waste. Unlike with freezing, food is not out of sight, out of mind. Food doesn't get buried in the bottom of a deep freezer and forgotten about well past its eat-by date, because people tend to store canned goods in often-accessed areas.

Pro of canning 6: It's the best way to preserve fruits. Canning is a fantastic way to preserve fruits and vegetables. Tomatoes and chili peppers do not freeze well at all but are great to jar under pressure. You don't even need to jar your tomatoes under pressure. You can water-bath jar tomatoes if you follow a recipe that has canning salt and vinegar.

THE CONS OF CANNING

Con of canning 1: It requires extra "spoons" and poses mobility issues. While most of the time spent canning is waiting for the canner to do its thing, more "spoons" are used during the process. They get used up preparing jars for canning, filling jars, sticking them in the canner, monitoring until pressure stage is reached to turn down heat, removing the jars from the canner, and much more—I'm tired just thinking about all this extra work.

While there isn't any bending involved with canning, it does require a bunch of time on your feet. This isn't something you can do while seated if you're using a stovetop pressure canner.

Con of canning 2: The upfront cost is high. Pressure canners cost over $100, plus there's the cost of canning tools and a bunch of jars to get you started. So, while you save a lot of money in the long term, you need to have the money to get started.

The Instant Pot Max would resolve a lot of the things mentioned in the first con, but its upfront cost is higher than that of a stovetop pressure canner.

Ultimately, there is no easy answer when it comes to canning versus freezing, especially as you can't jar everything, and you can't freeze everything. For me, canning outweighs freezing for a few reasons:

1. I can store way more precooked, ready-to-serve meals.
2. I don't have to think about what I want to eat at least a day in advance.
3. I have close to zero food waste.
4. While it uses more "spoons" than freezing, it doesn't hurt my body as much since there's no bending involved.

It's not about replacing one with the other; rather, it's about finding a balance between the two storage methods that works best for you when managing your disabilities.

CANNING STEPS

I *love* pressure canning as a method for food storage. It is safe and leads to less food waste. If you are using a stovetop canner, yes, there is the fear that it may explode. But after doing it a couple of times and becoming familiar with the manufacturer's instructions, that fear quickly disappears.

The pressure canner you buy will depend on physical limitations and whether you have someone living with you who is able to help with a huge stovetop canner. When I first started to can my food, my only choice was the stovetop canner, and I had to be able to use it on my own. As my disabilities increased in severity, my partner started to help.

Then, the Instant Pot Max was released. I can use the Max mostly on my own, but it has less capacity. Less capacity means more time needs to be carved out for canning. The only thing I need help with on the Max is removing the jars when the pressure has released.

Equipment:
- 23-quart (21.8 L) stovetop pressure canner or Instant Pot Max
- 5-piece canning set
- Plastic ladle
- Canning jars, snap lids, and screw bands certified for pressure canning

Time Under Pressure at 11 lb (76 kPa) of Pressure, Adjusting for Altitude

250 mL jars:
- Foods without meat: 45 minutes
- Foods with meat: 1 hour

500 mL jars:
- Foods without meat: 1 hour
- Foods with meat: 1 hour, 15 minutes

INSTRUCTIONS

1. While the electric pressure cooker is releasing pressure after cooking the food you wish to jar, fill your canning jars with hot water. Prepare your pressure canner with a little over the minimum required amount of hot water per manufacturer instructions and 2 tablespoons (30 mL) white vinegar. Place the pressure canner on low heat to keep the water hot.

2. Put the lids in a small pot and boil for at least 5 minutes.

3. Empty the water from the jars. Fill the jars with food, leaving 2.5 cm (1 inch) of head space. *Use a plastic ladle so that you don't risk introducing metal impurities or enamel into your food.*

4. Wipe clean the jar's threads. Add the lids and bands. Immediately place each jar in the pressure canner as it is filled.

5. Following the manufacturer instructions for your pressure canner, process per the above times, depending on contents and jar size, at 11 lb (76 kPa) of pressure, making any necessary adjustments for altitude. These adjustments are found in your canner's manufacturer instructions.

6. When it's done processing, remove the pressure canner from heat. Once the pressure has released from the canner, remove the jars, placing them on a tea towel to seal. You'll hear a popping noise as the lids seal.

7. If your jars do not seal, put them in the fridge and try again within 24 hours. If you are unable to try again within 24 hours, keep them refrigerated and eat the contents within 72 hours of the original cooking date. If at any time during processing the pressure falls below 11 lb (76 kPa) of pressure (or adjusted pressure for altitude), you need to restart the timer once it again reaches the correct pressure.

THE RECIPES

This book is more than a collection of recipes. Everything in this book is included to help you make your kitchen and cooking experience friendly for your disability. To get the most out of this cookbook, I highly recommend that you go back to the beginning and read each chapter before you cook your first recipe. In this way, you will get maximum benefit.

Each recipe also includes a few things not found in other cookbooks to help you in the kitchen. This includes storage methods, heat index where appropriate, what equipment you will need, a reminder to "mise en place" ingredients before getting to the method, and complete nutritional information to help you plan meals to ensure you get your daily vitamin, mineral, and macronutrient needs. (Mise en place is the fancy French way of saying "prepare your ingredients and place them in bowls in the order they will be dumped into the recipe.") Recipes also are sorted based on the amount of effort or "spoons" needed for prep.

Most recipes in this book take 20 minutes or less to prep. The prep times are based on how long it takes me to prep using a wheelchair and with limited ability to use my hands, and also on having to prepare ingredients before cooking rather than pulling something out of the freezer that's already prepped. You can reduce prep times by following the tips in "How to Meal Prep" (page 20).

Here are a few other bits of wisdom to help you get the most benefit when using this cookbook.

Electric Pressure Cooker Basics

Before you begin, be sure to read the materials that came with your cooker. Also, be sure to read the chapter on how to convert stovetop recipes into electric pressure cooker recipes (page 27). On top of all that information, I have a checklist to walk through when cooking in an Instant Pot, Ninja Foodi, or equivalent:

1. **Make sure there's at least one cup (250 mL) of liquids in the electric pressure cooker.** When doing this, remember that vegetables and meat release liquids as the cooker is coming to pressure, so sometimes you need to add only half a cup (125 mL) of water prior to cooking. But there are times, when steaming things, that you may have forgotten to add water and your pot says it's done. Then you find yourself cracking open what you think is a hard-boiled egg but it's still raw as can be.

2. **Make sure the sealing valve is closed.** I have a few cookers that have no manual sealing valve and three that do. On the Instant Pot Duo Crisp, quick release of pressure involves pushing down a valve that automatically pops back up when done. On the Max, quick release is done with a button, similar to setting the pot to High Pressure. But on the pots that have a valve, I have forgotten to reseal the valve after doing a quick release more times than I'd like to admit.

3. **Make sure Keep Warm is off.** You don't have to have ADHD to get distracted and forget about stuff happening in the kitchen. If you leave Keep Warm on, unless you are using a non-stick inner pot, you are inviting food to burn and stick to the bottom of the pot. The more viscous the food, the likelier it will burn.

   If you experience the dreaded burn and stick, add a couple of cups of water to the emptied pot, turn on to Sauté, and cook the food off. This is what is meant when a recipe indicates you need to deglaze the pot or pan.

4. **Don't forget to press Start if your cooker has a Start button.** There is a funny divide in my house. My partner with ADHD loves the Start

button because that step lets them know they've done everything they need to do, as they naturally do a mental checklist before pressing it. My autistic brain, which works on routine and automation, hates it. It's a huge adjustment for me to have to press a Start button on Instant appliances that have them. In our home we have four with a Start button. They are the Instant Pot Duo Crisp, Max, and Vortex Pro, and the Ninja Foodi.

No matter how your brain is wired, double-check that the Start button is pressed, even on appliances that don't have one.

5. **Don't use Delay Start.** I do not understand why there is a Delay Start. Using Delay Start can promote bacterial growth and lead to food poisoning. Cooking under pressure is not like cooking in a crockpot where you must start it before you leave for work if you want to eat at a decent hour.

If you work outside of the home and want to eat shortly after returning home, I recommend you prep before work and put it all in the fridge. Then dump and cook when you get home.

The only time I use Delay Start is when I'm cooking sides, for example steaming potatoes to mash, cooking rice by itself without meat, or steaming vegetables, and I'm attempting to time my dishes so that everything finishes at a specific time. But even in these circumstances, I am delaying by no more than one hour.

6. **Speed up the natural-release time.** Except when quick release is indicated, you need to allow the electric pressure cooker to naturally release pressure for at least 10 minutes. The natural release of pressure is part of the cooking process. You never want to use quick release in very full pots. Doing so creates a mess as food spews out of the valve with the steam. In these circumstances, to speed up the remaining natural-release time, place cold, wet dishcloths on the metal parts of the lid. You will probably have to wet them a second or even a third time, as all the water will evaporate. The evaporation process helps to cool the vapour responsible for the pressure inside the pot.

Pot-in-Pot Cooking

A couple of recipes in this book make use of this cooking method. It's a fantastic way to cook multiple dishes in one pot. An example of this is my Asian Fusion Japanese and Thai Peanut Chicken recipe (page 67). A few recipes in this book call for rice as part of the meal, which can be done pot-in-pot even if the recipe doesn't tell you to use this method.

I purposely left out pot-in-pot for most recipes that could be done that way because finding a pressure-safe container that can fit inside of the pot and leave enough room at the top may be an unmanageable added expense. If you're cooking rice using pot-in-pot, make sure the time under pressure is at least 10 minutes. Also be sure to cover the container holding the rice and water with aluminum foil.

Electric Pressure Cooker Cook Times Chart

A few of my recipes have ingredients that can be replaced with something else. For instance, you can use pork, beef, or lamb in my Chicken Dum Biryani (page 199). You can switch up which vegetables you use in my Thai dishes. In my Mexican Ground Beef Casserole (page 145), you can use dried kidney beans instead of canned if you add more water.

However, with a change in ingredients comes the possibility of a change in time under pressure. Here is a chart of cook times under the High Pressure setting so that you can not only switch up my recipes but also create recipes of your own. Remember, you cook according to the ingredient that takes the longest time to cook, and you don't need to increase time with increased volume. Also, the smaller you cut something, the less time it will take to cook.

Electric Pressure Cooker Cook Times

Vegetables

Asparagus		1–2 minutes
Beans	Yellow and green	1–2 minutes
Broccoli	Florets	1–2 minutes
Brussels sprouts		2–3 minutes
Butternut squash		4–6 minutes
Cabbage	Whole or wedges	2–3 minutes
Carrots	Whole or chunks	6–8 minutes
Cauliflower	Florets	2–3 minutes
Corn	On the cob or kernel	1–2 minutes
Mixed vegetables		3–4 minutes
Potatoes	Cubed	3–4 minutes
Potatoes	Whole, small	8–10 minutes
Potatoes	Whole, large	12–15 minutes
Sweet potatoes	Cubed	1–2 minutes
Sweet potatoes	Whole	12–15 minutes

Meat

Beef	Ground, including meatballs	4–5 minutes
Beef	Cubed	15–20 minutes*
Beef	Stew meat	20 minutes
Beef	Big cuts	20–25 minutes per 454 g (1 lb)
Chicken	Bite-sized cubes	5–6 minutes
Chicken	Whole breast/thigh, boneless	6–8 minutes per 454 g (1 lb)
Chicken	Whole (approx 2–2.5 kg)	8 minutes per 454 g (1 lb)
Lamb	Cubes	10–15 minutes
Lamb	Stew meat	12–15 minutes
Lamb	Leg	15 minutes per 454 g (1 lb)
Pork	Cubes	12–15 minutes
Pork	Roast	15 minutes per 454 g (1 lb)

*I've yet to find cook times for beef other than ground that works with a texture and flavour I can eat. It's always way overcooked. Don't be afraid to experiment.

Beans, Grains, and Legumes

Beans, black		Dry: 20–25 minutes Soaked: 6–8 minutes
Beans, kidney	Red	Dry: 20–25 minutes Soaked: 7–8 minutes
Beans, kidney	White	Dry: 25–30 minutes Soaked: 6–9 minutes
Beans, navy		Dry: 20–25 minutes Soaked: 7–8 minutes
Beans, pinto		Dry: 25–30 minutes Soaked: 6–9 minutes
Black-eyed peas		Dry: 14–18 minutes Soaked: 4–5 minutes
Chickpeas		Dry: 35–40 minutes Soaked: 10–15 minutes
Lentils	Green	Dry: 8–10 minutes
Lentils	Yellow and red	Dry: 1 minute
Rice, black	1:1 (rice-to-water ratio)	22–24 minutes
Rice, brown	1:1	20–22 minutes
Rice, white (basmati, jasmine, regular, etc.)	1:1	4 minutes
Rice, wild	1:2	20–25 minutes

About the Air Fryer Recipes

I love my air fryers. That said, an air fryer is not nearly as disability friendly as an electric pressure cooker because you can't just set it and forget it. Some babysitting needs to be done. And with some air fryers, you must turn the food halfway through to get an even crisp.

But there are a handful of oven and stovetop recipes that wouldn't work cooking under pressure that I can't live without. I have included these recipes in this book. They are as disability friendly as I could make them but do require a fair number of "spoons," especially executive-function "spoons" that get spent when having to watch over something.

If you want to adapt your oven or fried recipes for an air fryer, air fryer time is based on the same formula used for cooking in convection ovens: reduce the temperature by 25°F (4°C) and subtract 20 percent of the cook time. When using an electric pressure cooker–air fryer combo, you will need to add up to another five minutes. When cooking meat, it's always best practice to use a meat thermometer to determine when something is done.

Allergies, Food Intolerances, and Substitutions

There are a few ingredients used in the recipes in this book that you may be allergic to, have sensitivities toward, or just plain don't enjoy. It's okay to simply eliminate them. As an example, if you have a cumin allergy, don't include the cumin in Garam Masala (page 47), and simply use ground coriander in place of Thana Jeeroo (page 46).

If you are on a low-FODMAP diet for irritable bowel syndrome, use my Garlic- and Onion-Infused Oil (page 48) in place of garlic and onions, or just drop those ingredients altogether. Yes, it changes the flavour. No, it does not mean you are being untrue to the original recipe. For recipes that call for Ginger-Garlic Masala (page 44), replace it with half the amount of grated ginger or ginger paste. Remove onions and garlic after sautéing in recipes that use that preparation. Chives and the green part of green onions and leeks are low-FODMAP, so you can use a quarter cup (60 mL) of onion-family greens as a substitute for yellow or red onions. Prepared chickpeas, lentils, and mung beans are all low-FODMAP, so use them as needed. If, like me, you have that genetic trait that makes uncooked fresh cilantro taste like soap, omit it altogether.

If you want to use fresh dairy in place of coconut milk, do so. However, don't jar the food under pressure, as it will have too much dairy to do so safely. If a recipe has only a few tablespoons of dairy per 500 mL (pint) jar, it will be safe because those recipes still have a large amount of acid in them, making it more difficult for botulism to grow. But in recipes with substantial amounts of dairy, it becomes a lot more difficult to ensure that the entire contents of the jar reached the required temperature under pressure to kill all botulism spores. Food safety agencies around the world disagree with how much dairy is safe to jar, so it's best to err on the side of caution and freeze recipes with substantial amounts of dairy.

Reducing Spice: Flatbread Is Your Friend

There is a reason why naan—which technically is not a flatbread—roti, chapati, crackers, pita, and other forms of flatbread are typically served with Middle Eastern and South Asian food, other than being the primary utensil with which to eat. Taking a bite or two reduces the heat you may feel.

My favourite flatbread is roti. People who didn't grow up in communities with a large South Asian population typically don't know the joy of roti and why it's far superior to naan. It's not only easier to make but also cheaper and the best for cutting out heat. It's also the best to use as a utensil. And if you wanted, you could add some mild spice blends to the mixture before preparing.

The typical roti recipe is super easy and requires only four ingredients: flour, salt, oil, and water. The type of flour varies from household to household. Some use only whole wheat flour. Others use a mix of whole wheat and all-purpose flour. Still others use semolina flour. Rarely is any of it measured. It's all based on feel.

Simply add the desired amount of flour in a mixing bowl or bread machine. Add a teaspoon (5 mL) or so of salt. It's at this point that you also add spices if you so desire. Add a tablespoon or two (15–30 mL) of oil.

Blend. Add water, about a quarter cup (60 mL) at a time, combining after each addition, until it forms a nice ball about the consistency of homemade playdough. Let the dough sit for 10 minutes to allow the gluten to do some magic.

Once the dough has a chance to rest for 10–15 minutes, make balls about three centimetres (1 inch) in diameter. Then roll them into a circle. Brown on a hot skillet for about 1–2 minutes per side. To give it an extra something, you can put a trivet over a hot element, place the roti on top, and let it fill up like a hot-air balloon. Remove. Top with butter or ghee. Serve with your favourite meals, or freeze for later use.

The above way of telling someone how to cook something overwhelms a lot of different types of neurodivergent brains. But I told it this way to give an appreciation for how traditional home-cooked meals and sides are passed on from parent to child. And to illustrate that something delicious doesn't need to be complicated. Also, I wanted to honour that tradition, especially as I include a fair number of Panjabi recipes in this book.

Don't worry. There is a recipe that's easy to follow and takes out all the guesswork in the bread machine section (page 129). And if you don't have a bread machine, just mix it by hand in a bowl.

SPICE BLENDS
AND BASES

When it comes to cuisine, many South Asian words—more specifically Panjabi words, since that is the type of Indian food with which most North Americans are familiar—have been colonized, with their meanings being misused or misunderstood. It's important to me that when we eat foods from a culture to which we don't belong, we appreciate it and not appropriate it. In that spirit, here are four words that are commonly misused when talking about Indian food.

Chai: *Chai* means "tea." Don't say "chai tea" because you are saying "tea tea." The proper term is *masala chai*.

Masala: This means "spice blend." What westerners typically call "curry powder" is actually a masala powder. There is no such thing as curry powder. Curry isn't even a flavour.

Curry: This is a method of cooking. It means "to cook in a gravy." So if something has the word *curry* in it, it means that there is a rich gravy that includes a variety of spices and masalas.

Tikka: Oof, this one in particular gets me. Tikka masala is not an Indian dish. It was invented by white Britons who misappropriated both the word *tikka* and the word *masala*. *Tikka* means "marinated in spices," which makes saying "tikka masala" similar to saying "chai tea." It is, however, okay to say "chicken tikka" because this indicates that the chicken needs to be marinated before the dish is cooked. A lot of my Indian recipes are tikka curry, meaning the protein needs to be marinated and they are cooked in a gravy.

Ginger-Garlic Masala

Ginger-garlic masala is a staple ingredient in Indian cuisine. You always want to have a lot on hand in your freezer. Preparing it is easy, and it freezes wonderfully.

PREP:	TOTAL:		
10 minutes	10 minutes		
CUISINE:	**STORAGE:**	**SERVINGS:**	**CALORIES PER SERVING:**
Indian	Freeze, or refrigerate for up to 3 days	28 × 1 tablespoon (15 mL)	14 kcal

Gather Equipment:

- Cutting board
- Knife
- Garlic peeler
- Blender, food processor, or chopper attachment of your immersion blender
- Measuring cups
- Spatula
- ½-cup (125 mL) freezer containers

Prepare and Mise en Place Ingredients:

- 1 cup (250 mL) sliced ginger, unpeeled
- 1 cup (250 mL) garlic cloves, peeled
- 3 serrano peppers, seeded and chopped
- ½ cup (125 mL) water

Tip: When preparing meals, remove a container of Ginger-Garlic Masala from the freezer and stick it in your fridge the night before. Stores in the fridge for 3 days.

Variation: You may make this without the serrano peppers if you think it will be too much heat for your palate.

INSTRUCTIONS

1. Place all ingredients in a blender and blend until it is a purée or paste. You may need to stir occasionally to bring the unblended ingredients from the top to the bottom. Remember to always turn off the blender before removing the lid to stir.
2. Put the finished Ginger-Garlic Masala in ½-cup (125 mL) freezer containers. Label and freeze.

Nutrition Facts

Ginger-Garlic Masala
Per 1 tablespoon (15 mL)

Calories 14

Calories from fat 1

% Daily Value*

Fat 0.1 g	0%
Saturated 0.02 g	0%
Polyunsaturated 0.03 g	
Monounsaturated 0.01 g	
Sodium 2 mg	0%
Potassium 57 mg	2%
Carbohydrate 3 g	1%
Fibre 0.3 g	1%
Sugars 0.2 g	0%
Protein 0.5 g	1%
Vitamin A 5 iu	0%
Vitamin C 3.3 mg	4%
Calcium 10 mg	1%
Iron 0.2 mg	1%

*Percent Daily Values are based on a 2,000-calorie diet.

Green Chili Masala

This green chili paste is used in many Indian dishes. You can also add a teaspoon to any dish if you want to increase the heat.

PREP: 10 minutes	**TOTAL:** 10 minutes		
CUISINE: Indian	**STORAGE:** Freeze	**SERVINGS:** 21 × 1 teaspoon (5 mL)	**CALORIES PER SERVING:** 2 kcal

Gather Equipment:

- Cutting board
- Knife
- Measuring cups and spoons
- Blender, food processor, or chopper attachment of your immersion blender
- Spatula
- Silicone ice cube trays that make small ice cubes of roughly 1 teaspoon (5 mL), or a freezer bag

Prepare and Mise en Place Ingredients:

- 1 cup (250 mL) green chili peppers, such as serrano
- 2 tablespoons (30 mL) water
- ¼ teaspoon (1.25 mL) coarse salt

INSTRUCTIONS

1. Cut off the stems of the peppers. Place the whole peppers, water, and salt into the blender. If using a food processor, use the chopping blade.
2. Process until you have a paste.
3. Spoon 1 teaspoon (5 mL) of the paste into each cube in the ice cube trays and freeze. If you don't have small ice cube trays, put the paste into a freezer bag. Smooth out the paste until you have a thin, even layer, about 2.5 mm (¹⁄₁₀ inch) in height.
4. When needed, pop out an ice cube or break off a small piece of the chili paste.

Nutrition Facts

Green Chili Masala
Per 1 teaspoon (5 mL)

Calories 2

Calories from fat 0

% Daily Value*

Fat 1 g	2%
Saturated 1 g	6%
Polyunsaturated 1 g	
Monounsaturated 1 g	
Sodium 28 mg	1%
Potassium 15 mg	0%
Carbohydrate 1 g	0%
Fibre 1 g	4%
Sugars 1 g	1%
Protein 1 g	2%
Vitamin A 47 iu	1%
Vitamin C 2 mg	2%
Calcium 1 mg	0%
Iron 1 mg	6%

*Percent Daily Values are based on a 2,000-calorie diet.

Thana Jeeroo

Thana jeeroo—also known as dhana jeera—is an essential spice blend when cooking Indian food. *Thana* is coriander seeds. *Jeeroo* is cumin. In all recipes that call for Thana Jeeroo, you may replace it with half the amount of ground coriander and half the amount of ground cumin.

PREP:	COOK:	TOTAL:	
1 minute	16 minutes	17 minutes	
CUISINE:	STORAGE:	SERVINGS:	CALORIES PER SERVING:
Indian	Airtight container for up to 6 months	50 × 1 teaspoon (5 mL)	7 kcal

Gather Equipment:

- Measuring cups
- Frying pan and spatula
- Spice grinder
- Airtight storage container

Measure and Mise en Place Ingredients:

- ¾ cup (185 mL) coriander seeds
- ½ cup (125 mL) cumin seeds

INSTRUCTIONS

1. Heat a dry frying pan on medium heat.
2. Put the coriander and cumin seeds in the frying pan and lightly toast for 2–4 minutes, until fragrant and lightly browned. Be careful not to burn them.
3. Remove from heat and let cool for at least 10 minutes.
4. Once cooled, grind in the spice grinder for 1–2 minutes. Store in an airtight container or masala dabba.

Nutrition Facts

Thana Jeeroo
Per 1 teaspoon (5 mL)

Calories 7

Calories from fat 4	
% Daily Value*	
Fat 0.4 g	1%
Saturated 0.03 g	0%
Polyunsaturated 0.1 g	
Monounsaturated 0.3 g	
Sodium 2 mg	0%
Potassium 31 mg	1%
Carbohydrate 1 g	0%
Fibre 1 g	4%
Sugars 0.02 g	0%
Protein 0.3 g	1%
Vitamin A 15 iu	0%
Vitamin C 0.4 mg	0%
Calcium 20 mg	2%
Iron 0.9 mg	5%

*Percent Daily Values are based on a 2,000-calorie diet.

Garam Masala

Garam masala is an essential spice blend when cooking Indian food. Every home has its own variation of this blend. I highly recommend that you do not buy it in stores. If you do buy it in stores, don't buy it if it's red. That means it's primarily paprika, making it not garam masala but some colonialized something.

PREP:	COOK:	TOTAL:
2 minutes	2 minutes	4 minutes

CUISINE:	STORAGE:	SERVINGS:	CALORIES PER SERVING:
Indian	Airtight container for up to 6 months	25 × 1 teaspoon (5 mL)	10 kcal

Gather Equipment:

- Measuring cups and spoons
- Spice grinder
- Storage container

Measure and Mise en Place Ingredients:

- ¼ cup (60 mL) coriander seeds
- 2 teaspoons (10 mL) cumin seeds
- 1 teaspoon (5 mL) whole cloves
- 1 teaspoon (5 mL) cardamom seeds, from green or white pods
- 1 teaspoon (5 mL) ground cayenne pepper
- 4 bay leaves
- 2 sticks cinnamon, broken up

INSTRUCTIONS

1. Put all the ingredients in a spice grinder and grind, shaking every now and then to make sure nothing is stuck under the blades.
2. Store in an airtight container or masala dabba.

Nutrition Facts

Garam Masala
Per 1 teaspoon (5 mL)

Calories 10

Calories from fat 9

% Daily Value*

Fat 1 g	2%
Saturated 0.04 g	0%
Polyunsaturated 0.1 g	
Monounsaturated 0.4 g	
Sodium 2 mg	0%
Potassium 43 mg	1%
Carbohydrate 2 g	1%
Fibre 1 g	4%
Sugars 0.02 g	0%
Protein 0.4 g	1%
Vitamin A 50 iu	1%
Vitamin C 0.8 mg	1%
Calcium 20 mg	2%
Iron 0.7 mg	4%

*Percent Daily Values are based on a 2,000-calorie diet.

Garlic- and Onion-Infused Oil

Make this oil and use it in place of the oil, butter, or ghee and onions and/or garlic in recipes for a low-FODMAP version, while preserving some of the flavours. As an example, if a recipe calls for three tablespoons of extra-virgin olive oil and contains garlic and onions, replace the olive oil with three tablespoons of garlic- and onion-infused oil and omit the garlic and onions. If a recipe calls for three tablespoons of ghee and contains onions, substitute the onion-only version of the oil for the ghee and onions. Do the same with the garlic-only version if needing a substitute for garlic. While the recipe calls for half a cup of extra-virgin olive oil, it produces only about seven tablespoons since one gets lost in the process.

PREP:	COOK:	TOTAL:	
5 minutes	20 minutes	25 minutes	

CUISINE:	STORAGE:	SERVINGS:	CALORIES PER SERVING:
Many	Freeze, or refrigerate in an airtight container for up to 3 days	7 × 1 tablespoon (15 mL)	119 kcal

Gather Equipment:

- 3-quart (2.84 L) electric pressure cooker
- Cutting board
- Knife
- Measuring cups
- Oven mitts
- Silicone pot mat
- Fine-mesh strainer
- Stainless steel mixing bowl
- Spatula
- Storage container or ice cube tray

Measure and Mise en Place Ingredients:

Garlic- and Onion-Infused Oil

- 10 cloves garlic, sliced lengthwise
- 1 medium yellow onion, cut in eighths
- ½ cup (125 mL) extra-virgin olive oil

Garlic-Infused Oil

- 20 cloves garlic, sliced lengthwise
- ½ cup (125 mL) extra-virgin olive oil

Onion-Infused Oil

- 2 medium yellow onions, cut in eighths
- ½ cup (125 mL) extra-virgin olive oil

INSTRUCTIONS

1. Turn the electric pressure cooker on to Sauté. While it's still cold, add all the ingredients for the type of oil you want to make.

2. Heat until simmering, about 4–5 minutes. Press Cancel.

3. Remove the inner pot and put it on the silicone mat. Let the ingredients sit for at least 10 minutes.

4. Place the fine-mesh strainer in the bowl so that it is hanging. Pour the contents of the inner pot into the strainer.

5. Let the oil thoroughly drain into the bowl, about 4–5 minutes. When all the oil has drained, discard the contents of the strainer.

6. If freezing, spoon 1 tablespoon (15 mL) of infused oil per ice cube compartment. If storing in the fridge, use within 3 days.

Nutrition Facts
Infused Olive Oil
Per 1 tablespoon (15 mL)

Calories 119
Calories from fat 119
% Daily Value*

Fat 14 g	21%
Saturated 1.9 g	9%

*Percent Daily Values are based on a 2,000-calorie diet.

Herb Butter

You'll want to make this in advance of doing roast poultry to save on prep time. Freeze it and defrost it on the counter when you need it.

PREP:	TOTAL:		
10 minutes	10 minutes		
CUISINE:	**STORAGE:**	**SERVINGS:**	**CALORIES PER SERVING:**
Italian	Freeze	2 × ½ cup (125 mL)	868 kcal

Gather Equipment:

- Cutting board
- Knife
- Garlic press
- Stainless steel bowl, chilled
- Hand mixer, food processor, or stand mixer
- ½-cup (125 mL) storage containers

Prepare and Mise en Place Ingredients:

- 1 cup (250 mL) unsalted butter, softened
- ¼ cup (60 mL) chopped fresh rosemary
- ¼ cup (60 mL) chopped fresh sage
- ¼ cup (60 mL) chopped fresh thyme
- ¼ cup (60 mL) chopped fresh parsley
- 2 tablespoons (30 mL) minced or pressed garlic
- 1 teaspoon (5 mL) black pepper

INSTRUCTIONS

1. Put all the ingredients in a chilled stainless steel bowl and use the hand mixer to blend them all together.
2. Store in ½-cup (125 mL) storage containers.

Nutrition Facts

Herb Butter
Per ½ cup (125 mL)

Calories 868

Calories from fat 837

% Daily Value*

Fat 93 g	143%
Saturated 59 g	
Trans 4 g	369%
Polyunsaturated 4 g	
Monounsaturated 24 g	
Cholesterol 244 mg	81%
Sodium 21 mg	1%
Potassium 280 mg	8%
Carbohydrate 10 g	3%
Fibre 4 g	17%
Sugars 1 g	1%
Protein 3 g	6%
Vitamin A 4,299 iu	86%
Vitamin C 36 mg	44%
Calcium 205 mg	21%
Iron 5 mg	28%

*Percent Daily Values are based on a 2,000-calorie diet.

Chocolate Mint French Buttercream Icing

There are many types of icing for cake. My favourite type is a nice rich buttercream icing. This icing is to be used with my Chocolate Cake (page 111) if you want to create a dessert that tastes like a certain thin mint chocolate named after a certain evening hour. If freezing for later use, I recommend freezing it two portions per container, as the Chocolate Cake recipe makes two cakes.

PREP:	TOTAL:		
20 minutes	20 minutes		
CUISINE:	**STORAGE:**	**SERVINGS:**	**CALORIES PER SERVING:**
French	Freeze, or refrigerate for up to 1 week	8 × ¼ cup (60 mL)	309 kcal

Gather Equipment:

- 3-quart (2.84 L) electric pressure cooker
- Measuring cups and spoons
- Cutting board
- Knife
- Medium-large mixing bowl
- Whisk
- Hand mixer or stand mixer
- Microwave-safe glass measuring cup
- Microwave
- Silicone spatula
- ½-cup (125 mL) storage containers

Prepare and Mise en Place Ingredients:

- ½ cup (125 mL) sugar
- ¼ cup (60 mL) water
- ⅛ teaspoon (pinch) cream of tartar
- 1 large egg
- ¾ cup or 1 ½ sticks (185 mL) unsalted butter, softened and cut in 1 tablespoon (15 mL) cubes
- ¾ cup (185 mL) semi-sweet chocolate chips
- 3 tablespoons (45 mL) water
- 1 teaspoon (5 mL) mint extract

INSTRUCTIONS

1. Turn the electric pressure cooker on to Sauté. Add the sugar, the first amount of water, and the cream of tartar. Combine well. Be careful not to get any of the sugar crystals up the sides of the inner pot. Simmer until all the sugar has melted, about 2 minutes.

2. While the above is simmering, whisk the egg in the mixing bowl. If using a stand mixer, whisk the egg in the stand mixer's bowl.

(continued on next page)

3. While beating constantly with the mixer, slowly pour the contents of the inner pot into the whisked egg. Be careful not to get the syrup onto the beaters. Continue beating until the bowl no longer feels warm.

4. Add the butter, 1 tablespoon (15 mL) at a time, until smooth. **Note:** If the butter begins to separate because the mixture becomes too warm, refrigerate for 30 minutes, then resume.

5. Add the chocolate chips, the second amount of water, and the mint extract to the microwave-safe cup.

6. Put the cup in the microwave. Microwave until melted, about 30–45 seconds. Stir well. The chocolate should be glossy. Let the melted chocolate cool until lukewarm.

7. Using a silicone spatula, fold the melted chocolate into the buttercream until well combined.

8. Put the icing on a cake or freeze for future use.

ELECTRIC PRESSURE COOKER HUMMUS

There is a trend these days to misappropriate and whitewash food in ways I haven't seen in my lifetime. Hummus is one such dish. *Hummus* is Arabic for "chickpeas." Much in the same way that saying "chai tea" is inappropriate, saying "chickpea hummus" is also inappropriate. Labelling a blended dip/spread made from fruit as "hummus" is not only inappropriate—it is whitewashing. The full name of this dip is hummus bi-t-tahina, which translates to "chickpeas with tahini."

Electric Pressure Cooker Hummus

There are a lot of electric pressure cooker hummus recipes out there. However, a lot of them either call for the unnecessary step of soaking the chickpeas or add ingredients that make it no longer authentic to the region of origin. My Electric Pressure Cooker Hummus recipe cuts out presoaking the chickpeas and is made only with ingredients used in most regions of the Middle East. Also, cooking the chickpeas in the electric pressure cooker for the full 40 minutes adds a nice roasted flavour to them that is missing in other methods. If you want to add more ingredients to give it some extra flavours, go right ahead!

PREP:	COOK:	NATURAL RELEASE:	TOTAL:
10 minutes	45 minutes	10 minutes	1 hour, 5 minutes
CUISINE:	**STORAGE:**	**SERVINGS:**	**CALORIES PER SERVING:**
Middle Eastern	Freeze, or refrigerate for up to 1 week	1 × 1 cup (250 mL)	665 kcal

Gather Equipment:

- 3-quart (2.84 L) electric pressure cooker
- Measuring cups and spoons
- Cutting board
- Knife to smash the garlic
- Blender or food processor

Prepare and Mise en Place Ingredients:

- ½ cup (125 mL) dried chickpeas
- 1–2 cups (250–500 mL) water
- ¼ teaspoon (1.25 mL) salt
- 5 cloves garlic, smashed
- 2 tablespoons (30 mL) lemon juice
- 2 tablespoons (30 mL) tahini (sesame paste)
- 1 tablespoon (15 mL) extra-virgin olive oil

INSTRUCTIONS

1. In the electric pressure cooker, add the chickpeas. Cover with a couple of centimetres of water (minimum 1 cup/250 mL) and add the salt.

2. Place and seal the lid. Cook at High Pressure for 40 minutes.

3. Natural-release pressure for 10 minutes before quick-releasing any remaining pressure.

4. Remove the lid. Drain the chickpeas over a measuring cup to reserve ½ cup (125 mL) of the cooking water. Set the water aside.

5. Put the drained chickpeas, garlic, reserved water, lemon juice, tahini, and olive oil into a blender. Process until smooth, about 5 minutes.

6. Put the hummus in a container or serving bowl. It can be stored in the fridge for up to a week.

Nutrition Facts
Hummus
Per 1 cup (250 mL)

Calories 665

Calories from fat 324

% Daily Value*

Fat 36 g	55%
Saturated 5 g	31%
Sodium 85 mg	4%
Potassium 1,013 mg	29%
Carbohydrate 67 g	22%
Fibre 19 g	79%
Sugars 11 g	12%
Protein 25 g	50%
Vitamin A 67 iu	1%
Vitamin C 5 mg	6%
Calcium 147 mg	15%
Iron 8 mg	44%

*Percent Daily Values are based on a 2,000-calorie diet.

Electric Pressure Cooker Paneer

Paneer is a common source of protein in Indian cuisine. It is the Indian version of cottage cheese or cheese curds. Cooking under pressure is also common in Indian homes. A lot of Indian households make their own paneer because of ease. If you are vegetarian, you can use paneer instead of chicken and stay true to Indian cuisine.

PREP:	COOK:	NATURAL RELEASE:	TOTAL:
10 minutes	10 minutes + 2 hours at rest	10 minutes	30 minutes + 2 hours at rest

CUISINE:	STORAGE:	SERVINGS:	CALORIES PER SERVING:
Indian	Freeze, or refrigerate for up to 1 week	3 × 1 cup (250 mL)	637 kcal

Gather Equipment:

- 3-quart (2.84 L) or 6-quart (5.68 L) electric pressure cooker
- Stainless steel ladle (do not use a wooden spoon as it will harm the cheese)
- Cheesecloth
- Stainless steel pot or bowl
- Sieve or tofu press
- Something weighted, like a can of beans

Mise en Place Ingredients:

- 8 cups (2 L) half-and-half
- ½ cup (125 mL) white vinegar

INSTRUCTIONS

1. In the electric pressure cooker, add the half-and-half and vinegar. Stir.
2. Place and seal the lid. Set to Low Pressure for 10 minutes.
3. Natural-release pressure for 10 minutes. Quick-release any remaining pressure.
4. Remove the lid. Give the separated curds and whey a stir.
5. Drape the cheesecloth over a stainless steel pot or bowl. Carefully pour the contents of the pressure cooker into the cheesecloth.
6. Once all the curds are in the cheesecloth, grab the ends of the cheesecloth and twist it to extract as much whey as possible. You may store the whey for use in something else, such as homemade ricotta, or as a substitute for water when making bread, for added protein.
7. Place the cheesecloth with the curds in a sieve or tofu press. Place something weighted on top of the cheesecloth with curds. Let it sit for 1–2 hours to drain any remaining whey.

Air Fryer Matzo Meal

Matzo is an integral part of Passover. Coming by matzo, and matzo meal, outside of major city centres is near impossible without paying its weight in gold. Although its ingredients are simple, it is labour intensive. And if someone is keeping kosher, it needs to be made within 18 minutes after you've finished kneading the dough. Some interpretations of the Talmud say that someone may have up to 24 minutes before the matzo turns into chametz—leavened food forbidden during Passover—because of the yeast introduced from the environment, which contributes to the dough rising. Regardless, without a bunch of people on hand to help roll, perforate, and bake the matzo, keeping kosher for Passover when disabled can be daunting.

It took a long time, and trying a bunch of different tools, to develop a recipe that gets as close as possible to the strict 18-minute interpretation to keep this mitzvah, or Jewish commandment.

Please be sure to use measuring cups meant for baking. Your one-cup measure should be 236 millilitres. When cooking, you can use the metric equivalent of a cup (250 mL) for ingredients, but when baking, it's important to use imperial measuring cups and spoons, not metric. My kitchen has a mix of both, and I pull measuring cups and spoons specific for baking.

PREP:	OVEN-STYLE AIR FRYER:	COMBO-STYLE AIR FRYER:	TOTAL:
5 minutes kneading, 10 minutes rolling, pricking, and cutting	2–3 minutes	6–7 minutes	17–22 minutes

CUISINE:	STORAGE:	SERVINGS:	CALORIES PER SERVING:
Jewish kosher	Airtight container or vacuum seal	2 × 1 cup (236 mL)	574 kcal

Gather Equipment:

- 8-quart (7.57 L) electric pressure cooker–air fryer combo or oven-style air fryer
- Baking measuring cups and spoons
- Bread machine to knead the dough (optional; see instructions)
- Mixing bowl (if not using bread machine)
- Pasta roller or French rolling pin
- Fork
- Pizza cutter or knife
- 5-tier dehydrator rack for air fryer
- Blender or food processor

Mise en Place Ingredients:

- 2¼ cup (532 mL) all-purpose flour
- ½ teaspoon (2.5 mL) kosher salt
- 1 tablespoon (15 mL) extra-virgin olive oil
- ⅓ cup (80 mL) warm water
- ⅓–½ cup (80–125 mL) warm water

INSTRUCTIONS

1. In a bowl or bread machine, add the flour, salt, oil, and first measure of warm water. Knead until the dough is the consistency of damp sand. **Note:** If you need to keep kosher and don't have a pasta roller that attaches to your stand mixer or have only a French rolling pin, this is where the bread machine comes in. As long as it is being kneaded, the 18-minute stopwatch has not started on that dough. As a result, you may want to prepare the matzo in multiple rounds while the machine works the dough.

2. Slowly begin to knead in the second quantity of warm water. You want the dough to be very dry and not sticky, so you want just enough water to hold everything together. This can usually be done with only $\frac{1}{3}$ cup (80 mL) water.

3. Divide the dough into 8 balls. Flatten the balls to begin the rolling process.

4. If using a pasta roller, send the dough through at setting 8. Then send it through again at setting 4. Repeat with the rest of the balls. If using a rolling pin, roll the dough until it is only about a couple of millimetres thick.

5. With a fork, poke holes throughout the rolled-out dough, making sure to also poke holes in the edges so that the matzo doesn't bubble when baking.

6. With a pizza cutter or knife, cut each piece of dough into 6–8 pieces. Place the pieces evenly on the air fryer dehydrator rack, using only the bottom, middle, and top tiers. Place the rack in the air fryer.

7. Air fry at 400°F (200°C)—without preheating—for 2–3 minutes if using an oven-style air fryer, or 6–7 minutes if using an electric pressure cooker–air fryer combo.

8. Remove from the air fryer and let cool to room temperature.

9. Repeat steps 6–8 until all the dough is cooked.

10. Once it's cool, pulse in a blender or food processor until the meal is the consistency of coarse sand.

11. Store in an airtight container, or vacuum seal.

Nutrition Facts

Matzo/Matzo Meal
Per 1 cup (236 mL)

Calories 574

Calories from fat 72

% Daily Value*

Fat 8 g	12%
Saturated 1 g	6%
Polyunsaturated 1 g	
Monounsaturated 5 g	
Sodium 588 mg	26%
Potassium 151 mg	4%
Carbohydrate 107 g	36%
Fibre 4 g	17%
Sugars 1 g	1%
Protein 15 g	30%
Calcium 24 mg	2%
Iron 7 mg	39%

*Percent Daily Values are based on a 2,000-calorie diet.

LITTLE EFFORT

LOW PREP TIMES

Electric Pressure Cooker Tomato Coconut Soup

I didn't enjoy tomoto soup until, when I was living with the Sikh family, they served it with their special masala instead of salt and pepper. I fell in love with tomato soup and learned it can be made hundreds of ways that are unique to someone's cultural upbringing just by changing the seasoning choices.

PREP: 5 minutes	**COOK:** 5 minutes	**NATURAL RELEASE:** 10 minutes	**TOTAL:** 20 minutes
CUISINE: Indian fusion	**HEAT INDEX:** Mild	**STORAGE:** Jar at 11 lb (76 kPa) of pressure for 75 minutes	**SERVINGS:** 4 × 1 cup (250 mL)	**CALORIES PER SERVING:** 243 kcal

Gather Equipment:

- 3-quart (2.84 L) electric pressure cooker
- Can opener
- Food processor or chopper attachment for immersion blender
- Measuring cups and spoons
- Immersion blender or blender with a heat-safe container

Prepare and Mise en Place Ingredients:

- 400 mL (14 oz) can coconut milk, stirred
- 398 mL (14 oz) can no-salt-added diced tomatoes
- 1 red onion, chopped
- ¼ cup (60 mL) cilantro, chopped
- 1 tablespoon (15 mL) brown sugar
- 1 tablespoon (15 mL) Ginger-Garlic Masala (page 44)
- 1 teaspoon (5 mL) salt
- 1 teaspoon (5 mL) ground turmeric
- ½ teaspoon (2.5 mL) ground cayenne pepper

INSTRUCTIONS

1. Put everything in the electric pressure cooker.
2. Place and seal the lid. Cook at High Pressure for 5 minutes.
3. Natural-release pressure for 10 minutes, then quick-release any remaining pressure. Remove the lid.
4. Blend using the immersion blender. Do not use a blender unless your blender is rated for boiling-hot liquid and you follow the instructions if your heat-safe blender is glass.
5. Enjoy!

Nutrition Facts
Tomato Coconut Soup
Per 1 cup (250 mL)

Calories 243

Calories from fat 198	
% Daily Value*	
Fat 22 g	34%
Saturated 19 g	119%
Polyunsaturated 1 g	
Monounsaturated 1 g	
Sodium 740 mg	32%
Potassium 488 mg	14%
Carbohydrate 14 g	5%
Fibre 2 g	8%
Sugars 7 g	8%
Protein 3 g	6%
Vitamin A 288 iu	6%
Vitamin C 14 mg	17%
Calcium 60 mg	6%
Iron 5 mg	28%

*Percent Daily Values are based on a 2,000-calorie diet.

Electric Pressure Cooker Asian Fusion Japanese and Thai Peanut Chicken

This Asian fusion recipe that I created combines two of my favourite cuisines: Japanese and Thai. The thing people need to know about this recipe is that soy sauce is not used in Thai cuisine. As a result, this recipe is far more Japanese in practice than Thai. If you want to make it more on the Thai side, substitute fish sauce for the soy sauce. I like to use crunchy peanut butter for added mouth feel. It is a very disability-friendly recipe.

PREP:	COOK:	NATURAL RELEASE:	TOTAL:	
10 minutes	10 minutes	10 minutes	30 minutes	
CUISINE:	**HEAT INDEX:**	**STORAGE:**	**SERVINGS:**	**CALORIES PER**
Asian fusion	Mild	Freeze, or jar at 11 lb (76 kPa) of pressure for 75 minutes	4 × 1 cup (250 mL) with 1 cup (250 mL) rice	**SERVING:** 554 kcal

Gather Equipment:

- 6-quart (5.68 L) electric pressure cooker
- Measuring cups and spoons
- Cutting board
- Knife
- Stainless steel mixing bowl (or other oven-safe container) that will fit inside the pressure cooker
- Aluminum foil
- Trivet

Prepare and Mise en Place Ingredients:

- ¼ cup (60 mL) water
- ¼ cup (60 mL) soy sauce
- 2 tablespoons (30 mL) sugar
- 2 tablespoons (30 mL) white vinegar
- 1 teaspoon (5 mL) black pepper
- 1 tablespoon (15 mL) Ginger-Garlic Masala (page 44)
- 454 g (1 lb) boneless skinless chicken breasts (or thighs), cut in 5 cm (2-inch) chunks
- ½ red bell pepper, cut in thick slices
- ½ orange bell pepper, cut in thick slices
- ½ yellow bell pepper, cut in thick slices
- ½ cup (125 mL) peanut butter
- 1 tablespoon (15 mL) cornstarch
- ¼ cup (60 mL) cold water

For pot-in-pot rice:

- 1 cup (250 mL) basmati rice
- 1 cup (250 mL) water
- 1 tablespoon (15 mL) unsalted butter
- 1 teaspoon (5 mL) salt

Substitution: To make a vegetarian version of this dish, ideally you would want to use dried tofu. However, that can be hard to source, so substitute a full package of firm tofu, cut into cubes. The time under pressure remains the same. Ground cayenne pepper or fresh chillies, added to your desired heat, can be used in the place of the black pepper.

INSTRUCTIONS

1. In a bowl, add the first quantity of water, the soy sauce, sugar, vinegar, and black pepper. Stir until the sugar is mostly dissolved.
2. Pour the contents of the bowl into the inner pot of the electric pressure cooker.
3. Add the Ginger-Garlic Masala.
4. In the following order, dump in the chicken, bell peppers, and peanut butter.

For the pot-in-pot rice:

1. Put the rice, 1 cup (250 mL) water, butter, and salt in the stainless steel bowl. Make sure all the rice is submerged. Cover with aluminum foil.
2. Place the trivet on top of the chicken mix in the electric pressure cooker, and put the covered bowl of rice on the trivet.
3. Place and seal the lid. Set to High Pressure for 10 minutes.
4. Natural-release pressure for 10 minutes, then quick-release any remaining pressure.
5. Open the lid. Remove the bowl of rice and the trivet.
6. Turn the pressure cooker on to Sauté.
7. Mix the cornstarch with the second quantity of water.
8. Once the cooker contents are bubbling, stir in the cornstarch-and-water mixture. Stir until thickened.
9. Press Cancel. Serve the chicken on the rice and enjoy!

Nutrition Facts

Asian Fusion Japanese and Thai Peanut Chicken
Per 1 cup (250 mL) + 1 cup (250 mL) rice

Calories 554

Calories from fat 189	
% Daily Value*	
Fat 21 g	32%
Saturated 6 g	38%
Trans 1 g	
Polyunsaturated 5 g	
Monounsaturated 9 g	
Cholesterol 80 mg	27%
Sodium 1,681 mg	73%
Potassium 803 mg	23%
Carbohydrate 55 g	18%
Fibre 3 g	13%
Sugars 10 g	11%
Protein 37 g	74%
Vitamin A 1,068 iu	22%
Vitamin C 67 mg	81%
Calcium 46 mg	5%
Iron 2 mg	11%

*Percent Daily Values are based on a 2,000-calorie diet.

ELECTRIC PRESSURE
COOKER BUTTER CHICKEN

Butter chicken is one of my comfort foods. To be more specific, Panjabi food is a comfort food. As a teenager I was taken in by a Sikh family, and I can't live without Panjabi home cooking. However, I didn't grow up on butter chicken, as the dish would be invented years after local Sikhs first immigrated to the Cowichan Valley. Butter chicken doesn't originate in Panjab, though it is still Panjabi. The history of butter chicken is also a history of colonization; the dish was created to please Western palates.

Butter chicken was invented by Kundan Lal Jaggi. He was born into a Panjabi Hindu family, in what was Hassal, Jhelum, British India, which would become Jhelum, Panjab, after the violent partition of Panjab and Pakistan. This partition has resulted in intergenerational trauma, the effects of which are still visible today, as Panjabi Sikh, Hindu, and Muslim people were driven out of their indigenous homelands. Jaggi's story is one of these stories. The partition of India forced him to move to Delhi.

It was in Delhi that, in the 1950s, he would invent butter chicken through a tradition common in homes around the world: throwing leftovers into a pot and seeing the result.

Each of the Panjabi homes in my neighbourhood, including the Panjabi Sikh home I lived in for a time, had their own way of preparing a variety of curries, much like the origins of butter chicken. Each curry has a unique masala that was never measured out but made use of a base of common ingredients, adjusted based on smell.

Electric Pressure Cooker Butter Chicken

I've included this Butter Chicken recipe I developed to teach the basics of what a chicken curry can look like, to de-colonize a dish that was the result of colonization, and to teach an erased history for a dish that white people think is ordinary yet is anything but—even if the way it came to be is common in many traditions.

PREP:	MARINATE:	COOK:	NATURAL RELEASE:	TOTAL:
10 minutes	30 minutes (or up to 2 hours)	10 minutes	10 minutes	1 hour

CUISINE:	HEAT INDEX:	STORAGE:	SERVINGS:	CALORIES PER SERVING:
Indian	Mild	Freeze, or jar at 11 lb (76 kPa) of pressure for 75 minutes	6 × 1½ cups (375 mL) with ½ cup (125 mL) rice	743 kcal

Gather Equipment:

- 6-quart (5.68 L) electric pressure cooker
- 3-quart (2.84 L) electric pressure cooker or rice cooker
- Measuring cups and spoons
- Cutting board
- Knife
- Can opener
- Mixing bowl
- Plastic wrap
- Food processor or food chopper attachment for your immersion blender
- Wooden spoon

Prepare and Mise en Place Ingredients:

- 2 tablespoons (30 mL) Ginger-Garlic Masala (page 44)
- 2 tablespoons (30 mL) extra-virgin olive oil
- 2 teaspoons (10 mL) Garam Masala (page 47)
- 2 teaspoons (10 mL) Thana Jeeroo (page 46)
- 2 teaspoons (10 mL) salt
- 1½ teaspoons (7.5 mL) ground cayenne pepper
- 1½ teaspoons (7.5 mL) ground turmeric
- 900 g (2 lb) boneless skinless chicken thighs, cubed
- 398 mL (14 oz) can no-salt-added diced tomatoes, with liquid
- 1 medium yellow onion, chopped
- ½ cup (125 mL) water
- ½ cup (125 mL) unsalted butter, cubed
- 400 mL (14 oz) can full-fat coconut milk, stirred
- 156 mL (5.5 oz) can tomato paste
- ¼ cup (60 mL) chopped cilantro (optional)
- 1 teaspoon (5 mL) Garam Masala (page 47)
- 1 tablespoon (15 mL) cornstarch
- ¼ cup (60 mL) water

Rice:

- 1½ cups (375 mL) basmati rice, rinsed
- 1½ cups (375 mL) water
- 1 teaspoon (5 mL) salt

Substitutions: To make this vegetarian, substitute 3 cups (750 mL) cubed Paneer (page 59) for the chicken. Marinate it as you would the chicken. Change the time under pressure to 4 minutes.

You can replace the chicken thighs with the same amount of boneless skinless chicken breasts cut into cubes or use 680 g (1 ½ lb) precooked chicken or turkey without the skin. If using precooked poultry, you can reduce the time under pressure to 3 minutes, but note that even with the reduced cook time, using precooked poultry makes for dry poultry when jarred under pressure.

INSTRUCTIONS

1. In a bowl, mix the Ginger-Garlic Masala, the olive oil, the first amount of Garam Masala, and the Thana Jeeroo, salt, cayenne pepper, and turmeric.
2. Add the chicken cubes and mix until thoroughly coated. Cover it with plastic wrap and let it marinate in the fridge for at least 30 minutes but preferably 2 hours. **Tip:** On prep days, prepare big batches of chicken tikka (marinated chicken) and freeze it in recipe-sized portions. You don't need to defrost it on days you want a chicken curry. Simply add 5 minutes of time under pressure if cooking from frozen.
3. When the marinade is done, add the tomatoes, onions, and first quantity of water to a blender. Purée.
4. In a 6-quart (5.68 L) electric pressure cooker, add the purée and then marinated chicken. With a wooden spoon, spread out the chicken so that it makes an even layer.
5. Place and seal the lid. Cook at High Pressure for 5 minutes.
6. Natural-release pressure for 10 minutes, then quick-release any remaining pressure.
7. Once the pressure has released, remove the lid and turn on to Sauté. Add the butter, coconut milk, tomato paste, cilantro (if using), and the second amount of Garam Masala. Let it boil for 5 minutes to thoroughly denature the butter. Stir it often so that it doesn't burn.
8. Mix the cornstarch with the second quantity of water. Add the mixture to the electric pressure cooker and stir for a couple of minutes until it thickens.

For the rice:

1. In a 3-quart (2.84 L) electric pressure cooker, add the rice, water, and salt.
2. Place and seal the lid. Set to High Pressure for 5 minutes.
3. Natural-release pressure for 10 minutes, then quick-release any remaining pressure.

Nutrition Facts

Butter Chicken
Per 1 ½ cups (375 mL) + ½ cup (125 mL) rice

Calories 743

Calories from fat 396	
% Daily Value*	
Fat 44 g	68%
Saturated 26 g	163%
Trans 1 g	
Polyunsaturated 3 g	
Monounsaturated 11 g	
Cholesterol 184 mg	61%
Sodium 1,620 mg	70%
Potassium 1,108 mg	32%
Carbohydrate 55 g	18%
Fibre 5 g	21%
Sugars 8 g	9%
Protein 37 g	74%
Vitamin A 1,267 iu	25%
Vitamin C 18 mg	22%
Calcium 100 mg	10%
Iron 5 mg	28%

*Percent Daily Values are based on a 2,000-calorie diet.

ELECTRIC PRESSURE COOKER DAAL MAKHANI

One of my favourite things about Indian food is thali platters. *Thali* means "plate" or "full meal" and refers to the way Indian food is typically served. Every region of India has its own default of what is typically found on a thali.

In Panjabi cuisine, there are two versions. The first version makes use of a meat protein cooked using the curry method, usually chicken, with jeeroo rice, dry vegetables, a daal, cucumber raita, a dessert, and roti or chapati. The second version is vegetarian and usually consists of a chana (chickpea) dish for the protein, prepared using the curry method, to replace the chicken.

Daal makhani is now a common daal in Panjabi homes and restaurants when serving thali, thanks to its ease of making and ability to balance all the different flavour profiles. It wasn't always this way. Like butter chicken, this dish was invented by Kundan Lal Jaggi post-partition as a vegetarian alternative to butter chicken.

Electric Pressure Cooker Daal Makhani

The traditional recipe calls for cream. My version calls for canned coconut milk to help reduce food waste and to make it one of those dishes you can prepare any time without planning. The masala is also slightly different, but that's because every home has their own version of garam masala. My recipe calls for the use of either whole spices—if you have them—or two teaspoons (10 mL) of Garam Masala (page 47) if you don't.

PREP:	COOK:	NATURAL RELEASE:	TOTAL:
10 minutes	34 minutes	20 minutes	1 hour, 4 minutes

CUISINE:	HEAT INDEX:	STORAGE:	SERVINGS:	CALORIES PER SERVING:
Indian	Mild to medium	Freeze, or refrigerate for up to 3 days	12 × ¾ cup (185 mL)	209 kcal

Gather Equipment:

- 3-quart (2.84 L) electric pressure cooker (or a second inner pot for the 6-quart/5.68 L pressure cooker)
- 6-quart (5.68 L) electric pressure cooker
- Measuring cups and spoons
- Cutting board
- Knife
- Food processor or food chopper attachment for your immersion blender
- Can opener
- Wooden spoon

Prepare and Mise en Place Ingredients:

- 2 cups (500 mL) dried black beluga lentils
- ½ cup (125 mL) dried red kidney beans
- 4 cups (1 L) water
- ¼ cup (60 mL) unsalted butter
- 1 medium yellow onion, diced
- 1 serrano pepper, minced
- 4 teaspoons (20 mL) Ginger-Garlic Masala (page 44)
- 1 teaspoon (5 mL) whole cumin seeds
- 6 whole cloves
- 6 green cardamom pods
- 2 black cardamom pods
- ½ teaspoon (2.5 mL) green cardamom seeds
- 5 cm (2-inch) stick cinnamon
- 1 cup (250 mL) water
- 2 teaspoons (10 mL) salt
- 1 teaspoon (5 mL) ground cayenne pepper
- 398 mL (14 oz) can no-salt-added diced tomatoes with liquid, puréed
- 200 mL (7 oz) full-fat coconut milk (½ can), stirred

Tip: Black beluga lentils and whole spices can be difficult to source, but you can find them on Amazon.

INSTRUCTIONS

1. In the 3-quart (2.84 L) electric pressure cooker, add the lentils, kidney beans, and first amount of water. If you don't have a 3-quart (2.84 L) electric pressure cooker and are using two 6-quart (5.68 L) inner pots, do this step in the 6-quart with the first inner pot.

2. Place and seal the lid. Cook at High Pressure for 25 minutes.

3. Natural-release pressure for 10 minutes, then quick-release any remaining pressure. Set aside. If you are using two 6-quart inner pots, remove the inner pot and set aside. Then put the second inner pot inside the electric pressure cooker.

4. Turn the 6-quart (5.68 L) electric pressure cooker on to Sauté. Add the butter.

5. Once the butter is melted, add the onions, serrano pepper, and Ginger-Garlic Masala. Sauté until the onions are translucent, about 2 minutes.

6. Add the whole cumin seeds, cloves, three types of cardamom, and cinnamon stick. (If you don't have whole spices on hand, substitute 1 tablespoon/15 mL Garam Masala [page 47] for the whole spices, then proceed to Step 7 without tempering the spices.) Temper the spices until fragrant, about 2 minutes.

7. Press Cancel. In the following order, add the second amount of water, salt, cayenne pepper, and the puréed tomatoes.

8. Very slowly, add the lentils and beans with whatever water is remaining from steps 1–3. Be careful not to churn the contents to avoid a burn warning.

9. Place and seal the lid. Cook at High Pressure for 5 minutes.

10. Natural-release pressure for 10 minutes, then quick-release any remaining pressure.

11. Remove the lid. Stir in the coconut milk.

12. Enjoy!

Nutrition Facts
Daal Makhani
Per ¾ cup (185 mL)

Calories 209
Calories from fat 72

% Daily Value*

Fat 8 g	12%
Saturated 6 g	38%
Trans 1 g	
Polyunsaturated 1 g	
Monounsaturated 1 g	
Cholesterol 10 mg	3%
Sodium 403 mg	18%
Potassium 240 mg	7%
Carbohydrate 25 g	8%
Fibre 9 g	38%
Sugars 1 g	1%
Protein 11 g	22%
Vitamin C 6 mg	7%
Calcium 53 mg	5%
Iron 4 mg	22%

*Percent Daily Values are based on a 2,000-calorie diet.

Electric Pressure Cooker Tahdig

Tahdig is a traditional Persian dish that has so many different varieties. The word *tahdig* means "bottom of the pot." It describes the prized crispy layer of rice in this dish. Varieties of this dish cover nearly all the flavour profiles, including savoury, sweet, and sweet and savoury. It's a time-consuming dish to make when using conventional cooking methods.

   This is a sweet variety of tahdig. I decided to develop this recipe over a savoury yogourt variety to eliminate the need to prepare the rice twice. To achieve the results that come from conventional preparation in the oven or on the stovetop, the yogourt variety requires that the rice be cooked, removed from the electric pressure cooker so that the yogourt and butter can be prepared, then added back to the inner pot to be cooked under pressure yet again before the final sauté step. This recipe does call for saffron. Saffron is the most expensive spice because of how labour intensive it is to cultivate. If you can't afford the more expensive versions that don't make use of exploitative labour, then don't make the dish with saffron.

PREP:	COOK:	NATURAL RELEASE:	TOTAL:	
10 minutes	27 minutes	10 minutes	47 minutes	
CUISINE:	**HEAT INDEX:**	**STORAGE:**	**SERVINGS:**	**CALORIES PER SERVING:**
Persian	None	Freeze, or refrigerate for up to 3 days	7 × ¾ cup (185 mL)	399 kcal

Gather Equipment:

- 6-quart (5.68 L) electric pressure cooker
- Non-stick inner pot (optional)
- Measuring cups and spoons
- Cutting board
- Knife
- Mixing bowl
- Plate large enough to cover inner pot
- Rice spoon (optional if not using a non-stick inner pot)
- Wooden spoon

Prepare and Mise en Place Ingredients:

- ½ cup (125 mL) unsalted butter
- ½ teaspoon (2.5 mL) cardamom seeds
- 12 whole peppercorns
- 6 whole cloves
- Two 5 cm (2-inch) sticks cinnamon
- 1 medium yellow onion, thinly sliced
- ½ teaspoon (2.5 mL) saffron threads
- 2 cups (500 mL) basmati rice, rinsed
- ¼ cup (60 mL) diced dried apricots
- 2 tablespoons (30 mL) golden raisins
- 1 teaspoon (5 mL) salt
- 2 cups (500 mL) water
- ½ cup (125 mL) pistachio nuts, chopped

INSTRUCTIONS

1. Turn the electric pressure cooker on to Sauté. Add the butter, cardamom seeds, peppercorns, cloves, and cinnamon sticks. Sauté until very fragrant, about 3–5 minutes.

2. Add the onions and saffron. Sauté until the onions are translucent, about 3 minutes. (For a low-FODMAP version, remove the onions after sautéing.)

3. In a bowl, combine the rice, apricots, raisins, and salt. Add to the inner pot.

4. Add the water.

5. Place and seal the lid. Cook at High Pressure for 4 minutes.

6. Natural-release pressure for 10 minutes, then quick-release any remaining pressure.

7. Unseal the lid, then loosely place the lid so that it covers the inner pot without sealing.

8. Turn on to Sauté. Let it sauté undisturbed for 15 minutes.

9. Press Cancel. Remove the inner pot and put the plate on top of the inner pot.

10. While holding the plate tight to the inner pot, quickly turn the inner pot upside down to dump the contents on the plate. **Note:** If you are not using a non-stick inner pot, you will need to scrape the crispy rice from the bottom of the pot. Deglaze the inner pot by putting it back inside the electric pressure cooker. Add ½ cup (125 mL) water. Turn on to Sauté. Sauté while scraping the bottom of the pot to remove any remaining rice.

11. Sprinkle the pistachio nuts on top of the rice and serve.

Nutrition Facts

Tahdig
Per ¾ cup (185 mL)

Calories 399

Calories from fat 162
% Daily Value*

Fat 18 g		28%
Saturated 9 g		56%
Trans 1 g		
Polyunsaturated 2 g		
Monounsaturated 6 g		
Cholesterol 35 mg		12%
Sodium 345 mg		15%
Potassium 201 mg		9%
Carbohydrate 55 g		18%
Fibre 4 g		17%
Sugars 6 g		7%
Protein 6 g		12%
Vitamin A 623 iu		12%
Vitamin C 2 mg		2%
Calcium 62 mg		6%
Iron 1 mg		6%

*Percent Daily Values are based on a 2,000-calorie diet.

Electric Pressure Cooker
Thai Green Curry with Chicken

After Indian food, Thai food is the most agreeable to my stomach while also creating joy at mealtime. Most of the Thai food I ate when I was growing up was very colonized and made less flavourful. Then my youngest started to cook for an authentic Thai restaurant. He learned how to cook from the Thai owner, who would import a lot of the ingredients from Thailand as they are not easily found in stores. You have no idea what you are missing until you have the real thing.

Don't worry. You won't have to import any ingredients. I've kept the selection of Thai recipes I developed to ones that use ingredients that are easy to source in any store or can be ordered online. And while I developed this recipe using my knowledge of how heat sources affect flavour profiles, the flavours are very much true and authentic to the original source. For Thai curry paste, I recommend the brands Maesri or Mae Ploy. One 114-gram (4 oz) can of Maesri paste equals about six tablespoons (90 mL).

PREP:	COOK:	NATURAL RELEASE:	TOTAL:	
10 minutes	22 minutes	10 minutes	42 minutes	

CUISINE:	HEAT INDEX:	STORAGE:	SERVINGS:	CALORIES PER SERVING:
Thai	Mild	Freeze, or jar the curry at 11 lb (76 kPa) of pressure for 75 minutes and freeze the rice	4 × 2 cups (500 mL) with 1 cup (250 mL) rice	1,112 kcal

Gather Equipment:

- Two 6-quart (5.68 L) electric pressure cookers, or one 6-quart (5.68 L) electric pressure cooker and a second inner pot
- Measuring cups and spoons
- Can opener
- Cutting board
- Knife
- Food processor or food chopper attachment for your immersion blender
- Wooden spoon

Prepare and Mise en Place Ingredients:

For the rice:
- 1½ cups (375 mL) jasmine rice, rinsed
- ¼ cup (60 mL) black rice, rinsed
- 1 cup (250 mL) water
- 400 mL (14 oz) can full-fat coconut milk, stirred

For the curry:
- 1 tablespoon (15 mL) coconut oil
- 1 tablespoon (15 mL) Ginger-Garlic Masala (page 44)
- 1 medium yellow onion, diced
- 6 tablespoons (90 mL) Thai green curry paste
- 1 cup (250 mL) no-salt-added chicken broth
- 454 g (1 lb) boneless skinless chicken thighs or breasts, cubed
- 3 tablespoons (45 mL) fish sauce
- 2 tablespoons (30 mL) brown sugar
- 4 cups (1 L) frozen mixed vegetables
- 400 ml (14 oz) can full-fat coconut milk, stirred
- 2 tablespoons (30 mL) fresh Thai basil leaves (omit if you can't source)

Note: If using two inner pots, the cook time and the natural release time will each increase by 10 minutes.

Substitution: To make this dish vegetarian, substitute ¾ cup (185 mL) cashews for the chicken and 1 cup (250 mL) no-salt-added vegetable broth for the chicken broth. The time under pressure remains the same.

Tip: Black rice and Thai green curry paste are available online if you live in a food desert.

INSTRUCTIONS

For the rice:

1. In a 6-quart (5.68 L) electric pressure cooker, in the following order, add the jasmine rice, the black rice, water, and coconut milk. If using two inner pots with the same cooker, use the first inner pot.
2. Place and seal the lid. Set to High Pressure for 22 minutes.
3. Natural-release pressure for 10 minutes, then quick-release any remaining pressure.
4. Remove the lid and stir the rice. If using two inner pots, remove the inner pot holding the rice, cover, and set aside. Place the second inner pot in the electric pressure cooker.

For the curry:

1. While the rice is cooking, turn the second 6-quart (5.68 L) electric pressure cooker on to Sauté. Once it's hot, add the coconut oil, Ginger-Garlic Masala, and onions. Sauté for about 1 minute.
2. Add the curry paste. Sauté for a couple of minutes until very fragrant. Press Cancel.
3. In the following order, add the chicken broth, chicken, fish sauce, brown sugar, and mixed frozen vegetables. **Note:** Do not stir to combine. In dishes with small amounts of liquids, it is important to keep layers intact to avoid the burn warning.
4. Place and seal the lid. Cook at High Pressure for 5 minutes.
5. Natural-release pressure for 10 minutes, then quick-release any remaining pressure.
6. Open the lid. Turn on to Sauté. Once simmering, add the coconut milk. Stir and let it simmer for a couple of minutes. Press Cancel.
7. Add the Thai basil (if using). Stir.
8. Serve 2 cups (500 mL) curry with 1 cup (250 mL) rice.

Nutrition Facts

Thai Green Curry with Chicken
Per 2 cups (500 mL) + 1 cup (250 mL) rice

Calories 1,112

Calories from fat 522

% Daily Value *

Fat 58 g	89%
Saturated 47 g	294%
Trans 1 g	
Polyunsaturated 2 g	
Monounsaturated 4 g	
Cholesterol 108 mg	36%
Sodium 1,614 mg	70%
Potassium 1,456 mg	42%
Carbohydrate 115 g	38%
Fibre 15 g	63%
Sugars 15 g	17%
Protein 41 g	82%
Vitamin A 9,324 iu	186%
Vitamin C 29 mg	35%
Calcium 134 mg	13%
Iron 7 mg	39%

* Percent Daily Values are based on a 2,000-calorie diet.

Electric Pressure Cooker Spaghetti Sauce with Meat

Spaghetti sauce was the first "adult" recipe I learned, when I was thirteen. Getting it just right for this cookbook was hard. It took me a long time to crack this nut. Most electric pressure cooker spaghetti sauce recipes I have seen require ridiculous amounts of work, and you end up with a burn warning. A lot of the recipes don't even warn you that you will get the burn warning. Most are not even close to authentic Italian sauce. The things that make my sauce not 100 percent authentic are the use of beef for the meat, the addition of celery, and the omission of wine.

PREP:	COOK:	NATURAL RELEASE:	TOTAL:	
10 minutes	15 minutes	10 minutes	35 minutes	
CUISINE:	**HEAT INDEX:**	**STORAGE:**	**SERVINGS:**	**CALORIES PER SERVING:**
Italian	Extra mild	Jar at 11 lb (76 kPa) of pressure for 75 minutes	6 × 2 cups (500 mL)	234 kcal

Gather Equipment:

- 6-quart (5.68 L) electric pressure cooker
- Measuring cups and spoons
- Cutting board
- Knife
- Immersion blender with chopper attachment or food processor
- Garlic press
- Can opener
- Wooden spoon

Prepare and Mise en Place Ingredients:

- 1 tablespoon (15 mL) olive oil
- 454 g (1 lb) lean ground beef
- 1 small yellow onion, chopped or diced
- 3 stalks celery, chopped or diced
- 1 cup (250 mL) water
- 1 tablespoon (15 mL) Italian herb seasoning paste, or 1½ teaspoons (7.5 mL) dried
- 1 tablespoon (15 mL) minced or pressed garlic
- 1 tablespoon (15 mL) brown sugar
- 1 teaspoon (5 mL) black pepper
- 1 teaspoon (5 mL) salt
- 796 mL (28 oz) can crushed tomatoes
- 680 mL (23 oz) can tomato sauce
- 156 mL (5.5 oz) can tomato paste

Substitution: To make this dish vegetarian, replace the ground beef with the equivalent amount of your favourite ground plant-based product, like Impossible ground "beef." The time under pressure remains the same.

Tip: When cooking with ground meat, you want that to be the first ingredient in the pot with any aromatics and oil if applicable. Then add 1 cup (250 mL) water and make sure the pot is deglazed. Slowly add other ingredients, being careful to not churn. This is the best way to avoid the burn warning.

INSTRUCTIONS

1. Turn the electric pressure cooker on to Sauté. Once it's hot, add the olive oil, ground beef, onions, and celery. Sauté until the beef is crumbly, 3–5 minutes. Do not brown. You may season with a little salt and pepper when sautéing.

2. Press Cancel. In the following order, add the water, herb paste, garlic, brown sugar, black pepper, salt, crushed tomatoes and tomato sauce (slowly so as to not churn), and tomato paste. *Do not stir, or you will get a burn warning.*

3. Place and seal the lid. Cook at High Pressure for 10 minutes.

4. Natural-release pressure for 10 minutes, then quick-release any remaining pressure.

5. Remove lid. Stir.

Nutrition Facts

Spaghetti Sauce with Meat
Per 2 cups (500 mL)

Calories 234

Calories from fat 63

% Daily Value*

Fat 7 g		11%
Saturated 2 g		13%
Cholesterol 47 mg		16%
Sodium 1,417 mg		62%
Potassium 1,324 mg		38%
Carbohydrate 25 g		8%
Fibre 6 g		25%
Sugars 16 g		18%
Protein 21 g		42%
Vitamin A 1,190 iu		24%
Vitamin C 27 mg		33%
Calcium 92 mg		9%
Iron 6 mg		33%

*Percent Daily Values are based on a 2,000-calorie diet.

Electric Pressure Cooker Aloo Muttar Gobi Chana

This is a recipe that I created out of necessity, pulling on everything I learned growing up about cooking Panjabi food. I developed this recipe because I have a tough time meeting my daily protein and fibre intake needs in ways that are quick, convenient, and inexpensive. I have to consume much more protein than most people, nearly triple the recommended daily intake. There is only so much meat I can tolerate, even if I rarely eat beef, never eat pork, and consume mostly chicken and fish. Enter my love of pulses.

PREP:	COOK:	NATURAL RELEASE:	TOTAL:	
15 minutes	50 minutes	20 minutes	1 hour, 25 minutes	
CUISINE:	**HEAT INDEX:**	**STORAGE:**	**SERVINGS:**	**CALORIES PER SERVING:**
Indian	Medium	Freeze	5 × 2 cups (500 mL)	489 kcal

Gather Equipment:

- 6-quart (5.68 L) electric pressure cooker
- Measuring cups and spoons
- Cutting board
- Knife
- Vegetable peeler
- Strainer
- Bowl
- Wooden spoon
- Can opener

Prepare and Mise en Place Ingredients:

- 1 cup (250 mL) dried chana (chickpeas)
- 2 cups (500 mL) water (approx)
- 2 tablespoons (30 mL) extra-virgin olive oil
- 1 teaspoon (5 mL) cumin seeds
- 1 teaspoon (5 mL) coriander seeds
- 1 medium yellow onion, diced
- 1 tablespoon (15 mL) Ginger-Garlic Masala (page 44)
- 1 teaspoon (5 mL) Green Chili Masala (page 45)
- 1 cup (250 mL) water
- 2 cups (500 mL) frozen peas (muttar)
- 2 cups (500 mL) large-chopped cauliflower florets (gobi)
- 3 large russet potatoes, cubed (aloo)
- 398 mL (14 oz) can no-salt-added diced tomatoes, with liquid
- 156 mL (5.5 oz) can tomato paste
- 1½ teaspoons (7.5 mL) salt
- 1 teaspoon (5 mL) ground cumin
- 1 teaspoon (5 mL) ground turmeric
- 1 teaspoon (5 mL) ground cayenne pepper

Variation: If you think this dish will be too hot for your liking, omit the Green Chili Masala and ground cumin.

INSTRUCTIONS

1. In a 6-quart (5.68 L) electric pressure cooker, add the chickpeas and just enough water to cover them, about 2 cups (500 mL).
2. Place and seal the lid. Cook at High Pressure for 40 minutes.
3. Natural-release pressure for 10 minutes, then quick-release any remaining pressure.
4. Remove the lid. Pour the contents through a strainer, then place the chickpeas into a bowl and set aside. Put the inner pot back into the electric pressure cooker.
5. Turn the electric pressure cooker on to Sauté.
6. When it's hot, add the olive oil, cumin seeds, and coriander seeds. Sauté until fragrant, about 1–2 minutes. It's okay for the seeds to brown slightly, but don't burn them.
7. Add the onions, Ginger-Garlic Masala, and Green Chili Masala. Sauté until the onions are translucent, about 2–3 minutes. Do not brown.
8. Press Cancel.
9. In the following order, add 1 cup (250 mL) water, the cooked chickpeas, and the peas, cauliflower, potatoes, diced tomatoes, tomato paste, salt, ground cumin, turmeric, and cayenne pepper.
10. Place and seal the lid. Set to High Pressure for 5 minutes.
11. Natural-release pressure for 10 minutes, then quick-release any remaining pressure.
12. Remove the lid. Stir. Serve. Enjoy!

Nutrition Facts

Aloo Muttar Gobi Chana
Per 2 cups (500 mL)

Calories 489

Calories from fat 81

% Daily Value*

Fat 9 g	14%
Saturated 1 g	6%
Polyunsaturated 2 g	
Monounsaturated 5 g	
Sodium 1,099 mg	48%
Potassium 2,096 mg	60%
Carbohydrate 88 g	29%
Fibre 17 g	71%
Sugars 17 g	19%
Protein 19 g	38%
Vitamin A 1,219 iu	24%
Vitamin C 75 mg	91%
Calcium 151 mg	15%
Iron 8 mg	44%

*Percent Daily Values are based on a 2,000-calorie diet.

Electric Pressure Cooker Effin' Good Chili

I celebrated hard when I created this Effin' Good Chili recipe for the electric pressure cooker. I lost my family recipe years ago and had a tough time finding a chili recipe—either stovetop or electric pressure cooker—that I enjoyed. Finally, I found a recipe that most closely resembled the family recipe. It was for the stovetop, but with a few modifications in ingredients and method, I've adapted it for the electric pressure cooker.

PREP:	COOK:	NATURAL RELEASE:	TOTAL:
15 minutes	30 minutes	Full	45 minutes + natural release

CUISINE:	HEAT INDEX:	STORAGE:	SERVINGS:	CALORIES PER SERVING:
American	Mild to medium	Freeze, or jar at 11 lb (76 kPa) of pressure for 75 minutes	7 × 2 cups (500 mL)	511 kcal

Gather Equipment:

- 6-quart (5.68 L) or 8-quart (7.57 L) electric pressure cooker
- Measuring cups and spoons
- Cutting board
- Knife
- Food processor or food chopper attachment for your immersion blender
- Garlic press
- Can opener
- Small stainless steel bowl, chilled

Prepare and Mise en Place Ingredients:

- ¼ cup (60 mL) olive oil
- 1 medium yellow onion, chopped
- 1 large red bell pepper, chopped
- 2 jalapeno peppers, chopped, with seeds removed from 1
- 1 serrano pepper, seeded and chopped
- 4 garlic cloves, minced
- 900 g (2 lb) lean ground beef
- 2 beef bouillon cubes, crumbled
- ¼ cup (60 mL) Worcestershire sauce
- 2 cups (500 mL) water (or one 12 oz/355 mL can light beer and ½ cup/125 ml white wine)
- 2 tablespoons (30 mL) chili powder
- 2 tablespoons (30 mL) ground cumin
- 1 tablespoon (15 mL) brown sugar
- 1 tablespoon (15 mL) dried basil (or 2 table-spoons/30 mL fresh chopped basil)
- 1 tablespoon (15 mL) chipotle pepper sauce
- 1½ teaspoons (7.5 mL) smoked paprika
- 1 teaspoon (5 mL) salt
- ½ teaspoon (2.5 mL) black pepper
- ½ teaspoon (2.5 mL) dried oregano (or 1 teaspoon (5 mL) fresh chopped oregano)
- 796 mL (28 oz) can San Marzano tomatoes, with liquid
- 398 mL (14 oz) can fire-roasted diced tomatoes, with liquid
- 156 mL (5.5 oz) can tomato paste
- 796 mL (28 oz) can dark red kidney beans, drained and rinsed

For sour cream topping (optional):

- 1 cup (250 mL) sour cream
- 3 tablespoons (45 mL) chopped fresh cilantro
- ½ teaspoon (2.5 mL) ground cumin

Substitution: To make this dish vegetarian, replace the ground beef with the equivalent amount of your favourite ground plant-based product, like Impossible ground "beef"; replace the beef bouillon cubes with vegetable bouillon cubes; and omit the Worcestershire sauce. The time under pressure remains the same. Use regular paprika if you don't like a definite smoky flavour.

INSTRUCTIONS

1. Turn the electric pressure cooker on to Sauté.
2. When it's hot, add the olive oil. Let it heat for 1 minute.
3. Add the chopped onions, all the chopped peppers, and the minced garlic. Sauté until soft, about 1 minute. **Tip:** If you think this will be too spicy for you, omit the serrano pepper and thoroughly seed the jalapenos. If you want it extra spicy, leave the seeds in for all the hot peppers.
4. Add the ground beef, crumbled beef bouillon cubes, and Worcestershire sauce. Sauté for 3–5 minutes, just enough to make sure all the ground beef is separated. You don't need to thoroughly brown it.
5. Add the water (or beer and white wine) and deglaze the pot. Press Cancel.
6. In the following order, add the following, being careful to not churn: chili powder, cumin, brown sugar, basil, chipotle pepper sauce, smoked paprika, salt, black pepper, oregano, San Marzano tomatoes, fire-roasted tomatoes, tomato paste, and kidney beans.

7. Place and seal the lid. Set to High Pressure for 20 minutes. You can set it for as little as 10 minutes, but 20 minutes gives it a bit more time for all the flavours to set.

8. Allow the electric pressure cooker to naturally release all the pressure. *Do not do a quick release unless you want chili boiling onto the lid and in/out of the steam valve.*

9. Remove the lid. If you made your chili with alcohol, turn the electric pressure cooker back on to Sauté and let it boil for 5–10 minutes to burn off the alcohol. If you made your chili with water, you may want to do the same to boil off any excess water. Stir every few minutes so that it doesn't burn to the bottom of the pot.

For sour cream topping (if using):

1. While the electric pressure cooker is doing its thing, mix the sour cream, chopped cilantro, and cumin in a chilled stainless steel bowl. Cover and refrigerate.

Nutrition Facts

Effin' Good Chili
Per 2 cups (500 mL)

Calories 511

Calories from fat 252

% Daily Value*

Fat 28 g	43%
Saturated 10 g	63%
Polyunsaturated 2 g	
Monounsaturated 13 g	
Cholesterol 101 mg	34%
Sodium 1,031 mg	45%
Potassium 1,103 mg	32%
Carbohydrate 35 g	12%
Fibre 10 g	42%
Sugars 12 g	13%
Protein 34 g	68%
Vitamin A 3,000 iu	60%
Vitamin C 82 mg	99%
Calcium 160 mg	16%
Iron 7 mg	41%

*Percent Daily Values are based on a 2,000-calorie diet.

AIR FRYER SALMON AND PEAR SALAD

Salads don't always get the respect they deserve. In Western cultures, salads tend to be a bit on the bland and same-same side. In other cultures, salads have the full range of sweet and savoury, cold and hot, and multiple textures in one dish. More recent history has seen salads of Western origin introduced that borrow a bit from other traditions. An example is the Waldorf salad, which, while not strong in flavour, blends a bit of sweet and savoury with different textures.

My Salmon and Pear Salad is very much rooted in seasonal flavours of the West Coast but makes use of strong contrasts between sweet and savoury found in multiple cuisines, paired with a variety of textures that keep the mouth satisfied and curious about what surprises will unfold in the next bite.

Air Fryer Salmon and Pear Salad

While many of the air fryer recipes throughout this book have instructions for both the oven-style air fryer and the electric pressure cooker–air fryer combo, I'm including only the oven-style instructions here because using the combo appliance significantly increases the number of steps. These extra steps have the effect of increasing the cook time and the "spoons" required.

PREP:	OVEN-STYLE AIR FRYER:	TOTAL:		
10 minutes	5–7 minutes	15–17 minutes		
CUISINE:	HEAT INDEX:	STORAGE:	SERVINGS:	CALORIES PER SERVING:
North American	None	Refrigerate for up to 3 days	4	580 kcal

Gather Equipment:

- Oven-style air fryer
- Measuring cups and spoons
- Cutting board
- Knife
- 2 large mixing bowls
- Tongs

Prepare and Mise en Place Ingredients:

- Four 113 g (4 oz) skinless pink salmon fillets, about 2.5 cm (1 inch) thick
- Salt and pepper to taste
- 2 cups (500 mL) red grapes
- 1½ tablespoons (22.5 mL) extra-virgin olive oil, divided into ½ tablespoon (7.5 mL) and 1 tablespoon (15 mL)
- 2 ciabatta buns, cut in 2.5 cm (1-inch) cubes
- 2 green onions, thinly sliced
- ¼ cup (60 mL) full-fat Greek yogourt
- 2 tablespoons (30 mL) white wine vinegar
- 2 teaspoons (10 mL) sugar
- Two 142 g (5 oz) packages baby arugula and spinach mix
- 2 pears, cored and thinly sliced, divided in 4
- ½ cup (125 mL) crumbled goat cheese, divided in 4
- ½ cup (125 mL) chopped walnuts, divided in 4

INSTRUCTIONS

1. Prepare the salmon by seasoning it with salt and pepper to taste. Place the fillets on one of the oven-style air fryer's cooking racks.

2. Toss the grapes with ½ tablespoon (7.5 mL) of the olive oil. Place them on the same cooking rack as the salmon.

3. Toss the ciabatta cubes with the remaining 1 tablespoon (15 mL) of olive oil and salt and pepper to taste. Place them on the other cooking rack. **Note:** If you can't fit all the salmon and grapes on the first rack, you can also place grapes on this rack. Just note that you will be removing the croutons partway through the cooking process, so place the items accordingly.

4. Using the Bake function, set the oven-style air fryer to 400°F (200°C) for 4 minutes. Let the oven preheat.

5. When the Add Food indicator goes off, place the salmon and grapes on the bottom rung and the ciabatta cubes on the top.

6. Air fry for 3–4 minutes until the croutons are golden brown.

7. Remove the now finished croutons.

8. Using the Bake function, reset the air fryer to 400°F (200°C) for 3 minutes. Without waiting for it to preheat, air fry the salmon and grapes for an additional 2–3 minutes, until the salmon is done. There are two ways you can determine if the salmon is done. Stick a meat probe into the middle of the salmon from the side; the temperature should read 145°F (63°C). Alternatively, cut the salmon in half; the salmon is done if the colour is the same throughout.

9. In a large mixing bowl, combine the green onions, yogourt, vinegar, and sugar. Add to the salad mix and toss.

10. Divide the tossed salad greens among four plates.

11. Top with the grapes, croutons, salmon, and pear slices.

12. Sprinkle with the goat cheese and walnuts. Enjoy!

Nutrition Facts

Salmon and Pear Salad
Per 1 salad

Calories 580

Calories from fat 261

% Daily Value*

Fat 29 g	45%
Saturated 7 g	44%
Polyunsaturated 11 g	
Monounsaturated 9 g	
Cholesterol 76 mg	25%
Sodium 338 mg	15%
Potassium 1,239 mg	35%
Carbohydrate 48 g	16%
Fibre 6 g	25%
Sugars 24 g	27%
Protein 36 g	72%
Vitamin A 4,645 iu	93%
Vitamin C 23 mg	28%
Calcium 194 mg	19%
Iron 4 mg	22%

*Percent Daily Values are based on a 2,000-calorie diet.

Air Fryer Chicken Pakora

One of my favourite snacks is chicken pakora. Because of the amount of time needed standing over a pot with spitting hot oil on the stove, it isn't the most disability-friendly thing to make for people with mobility issues. Thankfully, after some experimenting, I was able to adapt a recipe—passed on to me—for the air fryer.

PREP:	OVEN-STYLE AIR FRYER:	COMBO-STYLE AIR FRYER:	TOTAL:	
15 minutes	4–6 minutes	12–14 minutes	19–29 minutes	
CUISINE:	HEAT INDEX:	STORAGE:	SERVINGS:	CALORIES PER SERVING:
Indian	Mild to medium	Freeze	6	273 kcal

Gather Equipment:

- 8-quart (7.57 L) electric pressure cooker–air fryer combo or oven-style air fryer
- Cutting board
- Knife
- Measuring cups and spoons
- Mixing bowls
- Mixing spoons or spatulas
- Pastry blender or fork
- Parchment paper
- Trivet
- Bottom of a 6-to-8-inch (15–20 cm) round springform pan
- Pastry brush or paper towel
- Tongs

Prepare and Mise en Place Ingredients:

For the marinade:

- 454 g (1 lb) boneless skinless chicken thighs
- 1 tablespoon (15 mL) olive oil
- 2 teaspoons (10 mL) minced garlic
- 1 teaspoon (5 mL) ground turmeric
- 1 teaspoon (5 mL) Thana Jeeroo (page 46)
- ½ teaspoon (2.5 mL) ground cayenne pepper
- ½ teaspoon (2.5 mL) Garam Masala (page 47)
- ½ teaspoon (2.5 mL) salt

For the pakora batter:

- 1 ¼ cups (300 mL) chana (chickpea) flour
- 3 tablespoons (45 mL) vegetable oil
- 1 ½ teaspoons (7.5 mL) Ginger-Garlic Masala (page 44)
- 1 teaspoon (5 ml) Garam Masala (page 47)
- 1 teaspoon (5 ml) Thana Jeeroo (page 46)
- 1 teaspoon (5 mL) salt
- ½ teaspoon (2.5 mL) ground cayenne pepper
- ½ teaspoon (2.5 mL) Green Chili Masala (page 45)
- ¼ teaspoon (1.25 mL) ground turmeric
- Whole cumin seeds, to taste (optional)
- ¾–1 cup (185–250 mL) water
- Vegetable oil for brushing air fryer racks

Substitution: To make this dish vegetarian, substitute steamed potato wedges for the chicken and air fry per the instructions. If you want to use raw potato wedges, increase the air-frying time to 15 minutes for the oven-style air fryer and 20 minutes for the electric pressure cooker–air fryer combo.

INSTRUCTIONS

For the marinade:

1. Cut the chicken thighs into thin strips, 1 cm (½ inch) wide and 5–7.5 cm (2–3 inches) long.

2. In a mixing bowl, combine the olive oil, garlic, turmeric, Thana Jeeroo, cayenne pepper, Garam Masala, and salt to make a paste.

3. Add the chicken strips to the paste. Mix well until the chicken is evenly coated. Set aside. Do not refrigerate.

For the pakora batter:

1. In a bowl, use a pastry blender or fork to mix the flour, oil, Ginger-Garlic Masala, Garam Masala, Thana Jeeroo, salt, cayenne pepper, Green Chili Masala, and turmeric. Blend the flour until it clumps and looks like chickpeas again. If you want an extra kick in your pakora, also add whole cumin seeds, to taste.

2. Little by little, add the water while mixing to form a batter with a consistency somewhere between waffle batter and thick pancake batter.

3. Add the marinated chicken to the batter. Stir until all the chicken is thoroughly coated.

If using an electric pressure cooker–air fryer combo:

1. Place parchment paper at the bottom of the inner pot to make cleanup easier. Place the trivet with the springform pan on top of the parchment paper.

2. Lightly brush the springform pan with vegetable oil. Using tongs, place chicken strips in a single layer.

3. Place the air fryer lid. Air fry at 400°F (200°C) for 12–14 minutes. To test if the pakoras are done, tear one in half. If it's not done, air fry for a couple more minutes.

4. Remove the cooked pakoras from the air fryer. Clean the rack. Repeat steps 1–3 until all the pakoras are done.

If using an oven-style air fryer:

1. Place parchment paper under the air fryer racks to catch the drips during placement of the pakoras.

2. With parchment paper under the two racks, lightly brush the racks with vegetable oil.

3. Using tongs, add the chicken to the frying racks in an even, single layer.

4. Place the racks inside the air fryer.

5. Close the door. Using the Bake function, air fry at 400°F (200°C) for 4–6 minutes. To test if the pakoras are done, tear one in half. If it's not done, air fry for a couple more minutes.

6. Enjoy!

Nutrition Facts

Chicken Pakora
Per serving

Calories 273

Calories from fat 126	
% Daily Value*	
Fat 14 g	22%
Saturated 7 g	44%
Polyunsaturated 1 g	
Monounsaturated 1 g	
Cholesterol 72 mg	24%
Sodium 670 mg	29%
Potassium 413 mg	12%
Carbohydrate 15 g	5%
Fibre 3 g	13%
Sugars 3 g	3%
Protein 20 g	40%
Vitamin A 153 iu	3%
Vitamin C 1 mg	1%
Calcium 23 mg	2%
Iron 3 mg	17%

*Percent Daily Values are based on a 2,000-calorie diet.

AIR FRYER MASALA SHORTBREAD

My Air Fryer Masala Shortbread cookies are a delicious savoury snack that melts in your mouth and has 25 percent of our daily recommended fibre.

Developing this recipe was especially important to me. Like some, I have reactive hypoglycemia. I love to do light exercise that involves sitting on a yoga ball, bouncing away while doing the arm movements in *Just Dance*. As I got older, I started to experience a huge sugar crash after I did anything that put my heart rate into the cardio zone for more than 10 minutes. This resulted in a migraine with loss of vision. Finding things to eat quickly that don't involve me shovelling full-fat Greek yogourt with a piece of fruit into my face while I'm bending over the kitchen sink is difficult.

I also have IBS-M, a type of irritable bowel syndrome, which makes fibre tricky. Getting enough fibre while finding the perfect balance between insoluble and soluble fibre sources is tough work.

Air Fryer Masala Shortbread

I came up with the idea to do this savoury Air Fryer Masala Shortbread using a good source of fibre, lots of fats to combat a crash due to too many carbs, and a flour with a higher protein source than regular white flour. If you pair my Masala Shortbread with a nice source of protein, it makes a great, satiating snack, thanks to the fat-fibre-protein combo.

PREP:	OVEN-STYLE AIR FRYER:	TOTAL:		
15 minutes	30–35 minutes	45–50 minutes		

CUISINE:	HEAT INDEX:	STORAGE:	SERVINGS:	CALORIES PER SERVING:
Fusion	Mild	Freeze	8 × 3 cookies	277 kcal

Gather Equipment:

- Oven-style air fryer
- 8- × 8-inch (20 × 20 cm) baking tin or whatever fits in your air fryer
- Measuring cups and spoons
- Cutting board
- Knife
- Mixing bowls
- Stand mixer, hand mixer, or food processor
- Fork
- Cooling rack

Prepare and Mise en Place Ingredients:

- ¾ cup (180 mL) unsalted butter, cubed and softened
- 3 tablespoons (45 mL) icing sugar
- 3 tablespoons (45 mL) granulated sugar
- 2 tablespoons (30 mL) full-fat Greek yogourt (at least 4 percent milk fat)
- 1 teaspoon (5 mL) ground ginger
- 1 teaspoon (5 mL) Garam Masala (page 47)
- ½ teaspoon (2.5 mL) ground turmeric
- ¼ teaspoon (1.25 mL) salt
- ¼ teaspoon (1.25 mL) ground cáyenne pepper
- 1 cup (236 mL) semolina flour
- ¼ cup (60 mL) oat fibre (can be purchased online)
- ¼ cup (60 mL) cornstarch

Tip: If you want to make these in the oven, preheat your oven to 300°F (150°C). Bake for 45–50 minutes, until the edges move away from the sides of the tin.

You may enjoy these Masala Shortbread cookies on their own or paired with smoked seafood, shredded chicken, cheese, mushrooms, or any other protein you enjoy for snacks.

INSTRUCTIONS

1. In the bowl of your stand mixer or food processor or a mixing bowl, add the cubes of butter, both types of sugar, Greek yogourt, ginger, Garam Masala, turmeric, salt, and cayenne pepper. Blend thoroughly, about 5 minutes.

2. In a mixing bowl, combine the flour, oat fibre, and cornstarch.

3. With the stand mixer, hand mixer, or food processor still going, add the flour mixture ¼ cup (60 mL) at a time until everything is thoroughly blended.

4. In your baking tin, add the dough in an even layer. With a fork, poke holes evenly throughout.

5. Using the Bake setting, set the air fryer to 300°F (150°C) for 35 minutes. Let the oven preheat.

6. When the air fryer's Add Food indicator goes off, put the baking tin on the bottom rack. Air fry for 30–35 minutes, until the edges begin to separate from the sides of the tin.

7. When done, remove from the air fryer. Cut into 24 pieces.

8. Remove the cookies from the tin and place them on a cooling rack.

Nutrition Facts

Masala Shortbread
Per 3 cookies

Calories 277

Calories from fat 162

% Daily Value*

Fat 18 g		28%
Saturated 11 g		69%
Polyunsaturated 1 g		
Monounsaturated 5 g		
Cholesterol 46 mg		15%
Sodium 77 mg		3%
Potassium 63 mg		2%
Carbohydrate 27 g		9%
Fibre 6 g		25%
Sugars 8 g		9%
Protein 3 g		6%
Vitamin A 562 iu		11%
Vitamin C 1 mg		1%
Calcium 16 mg		2%
Iron 1 mg		6%

*Percent Daily Values are based on a 2,000-calorie diet.

Air Fryer Chocolate Cake

Developing this recipe became like a mission impossible for me. Every cookbook needs a cake. And I was determined to create an air fryer cake that was moist and evenly risen. Cooking cake in an electric pressure cooker is simple. However, the moisture from that process creates a cake that's a little bit dense, even if very moist. I was really missing that oven-baked feeling in my mouth. With my mobility-related disabilities, cooking in the oven is now a no-go without an assistant, and when craving cake, no one wants to wait around for someone to be available to help.

The secret to cracking this code included using less flour than called for in traditional methods, making use of full-fat Greek yogourt, and wrapping the springform cake pans in moist paper towel. Do not skip the paper towel step if you want an amazing cake! This is the most vital step to make a cake that doesn't have a hard shell and rises evenly.

PREP:	OVEN-STYLE AIR FRYER:	COMBO-STYLE AIR FRYER:	TOTAL:
15 minutes	22–24 minutes	25–27 minutes	37–42 minutes

CUISINE:	STORAGE:	SERVINGS:	CALORIES PER SERVING:
Multiple	Eat within 3 days or freeze	4 × half a 4-inch (10 cm) round cake	319 kcal

Gather Equipment:

- Oven-style air fryer or electric pressure cooker–air fryer combo
- Measuring cups and spoons
- 2 mixing bowls
- Electric hand mixer or stand mixer
- Two 4-inch (10 cm) springform cake pans
- Non-stick cooking spray
- Spatula
- Select-a-size paper towel
- Trivet if using an electric pressure cooker–air fryer combo
- Toothpicks

Prepare and Mise en Place Ingredients:

- ½ cup (120 mL) sugar
- ¼ cup (60 mL) unsalted butter, softened
- 1 large egg, room temperature
- ¼ cup (60 mL) full-fat Greek yogourt
- ⅔ cup (160 mL) all-purpose flour
- ¼ cup (60 mL) cocoa powder
- ¼ teaspoon (1.25 mL) baking soda
- ¼ teaspoon (1.25 mL) salt
- ¼ cup (60 mL) 2 percent milk

INSTRUCTIONS

1. Using the hand mixer or stand mixer, in a mixing bowl, cream the sugar and butter.
2. Add the egg and yogourt. Mix until smooth.
3. In another mixing bowl, add the flour, cocoa powder, baking soda, and salt. Combine well.
4. In the mixing bowl with the wet mixture, add half of the dry ingredients. Using the hand mixer or stand mixer, mix until well combined.
5. To the mixture in step 4, add half of the milk. Mix until well combined.
6. Repeat steps 4 and 5.

7. Spray both springform pans with non-stick cooking spray. Fill each pan half-way with the cake batter.

8. Grab 4 sections of select-a-size paper towel. Wet the towels so that they are very damp but not dripping. Fold the towels into thirds. Wrap the towels around each springform pan so that the pans are completely wrapped in damp paper towel.

9. **If using an oven-style air fryer:** Using the Bake function, set the air fryer to 325°F (165°C) for 22 minutes. Let the oven preheat. **If using an electric pressure cooker–air fryer combo:** Put the trivet in the air fryer. Put the springform pans on the trivet. Place the lid.

10. **If using an oven-style air fryer:** When the air fryer's Add Food indicator goes off, insert the wrapped springform pans on the bottom rack and bake until the Done alarm sounds. **If using an electric pressure cooker–air fryer combo:** Using the Bake function, air fry at 325°F (165°C) for 25 minutes.

11. Remove the cake from the air fryer. To test if it's done, insert a toothpick into the centre of the cake. The toothpick should be clean when removed. If the toothpick isn't clean, bake for another 1–2 minutes.

Nutrition Facts

Chocolate Cake
Per half a 4-inch (10 cm) cake

Calories 319

Calories from fat 126	
% Daily Value*	
Fat 14 g	22%
Saturated 8 g	50%
Trans 1 g	
Polyunsaturated 1 g	
Monounsaturated 4 g	
Cholesterol 79 mg	26%
Sodium 246 mg	11%
Potassium 164 mg	5%
Carbohydrate 45 g	15%
Fibre 2 g	8%
Sugars 26 g	29%
Protein 7 g	14%
Vitamin A 438 iu	9%
Vitamin C 1 mg	1%
Calcium 52 mg	5%
Iron 2 mg	11%

*Percent Daily Values are based on a 2,000-calorie diet.

Air Fryer and Electric Pressure Cooker Thai Winter Squash Soup

One of the things I love about autumn and winter is the abundance of different types of squash available, including less-used varieties such as mashed potato squash (yes, there is a winter squash that tastes nearly identical to mashed potatoes). With this season comes autumnal soups. One of my favourite soups to make with squash is Thai Winter Squash Soup.

My recipe makes use of the traditional base of different salts and acids that form the foundation of many Thai dishes. The type of squash you use is entirely up to you. My preference is to use a sweet pumpkin about the size of an acorn squash and a mashed potato squash. Acorn squash also makes for a great version. You can use any type you like as long as it's about the size of an acorn squash.

PREP:	COOK:	NATURAL RELEASE:	TOTAL:	
15 minutes	35 minutes	10 minutes	1 hour	
CUISINE:	HEAT INDEX:	STORAGE:	SERVINGS:	CALORIES PER SERVING:
Thai	Medium to high	Freeze, or refrigerate for up to 3 days	6 × 1½ cups (375 mL)	344 kcal

Gather Equipment:

- Oven-style air fryer
- Oil brush
- Soup spoon
- Large bowl
- 6-quart (5.68 L) electric pressure cooker
- Measuring cups and spoons
- Cutting board
- Knife
- Spatula
- Wooden spoon
- Can opener
- Immersion blender or heat-safe blender
- Storage containers if freezing

Prepare and Mise en Place Ingredients:

- 2 winter squash, cut in half
- 2 tablespoons (30 mL) extra-virgin olive oil (approx)
- 1 teaspoon (5 mL) finishing salt (or to taste)
- 1 tablespoon (15 mL) extra-virgin olive oil
- ¼ cup (60 mL) Ginger-Garlic Masala (page 44)
- 1 medium yellow onion, chopped
- 4 tablespoons (60 mL) Thai red curry paste (use less for milder heat)
- 2 cups (500 mL) no-salt-added chicken broth or vegetable broth
- ¼ cup (60 mL) fish sauce
- 2 tablespoons (30 mL) brown sugar
- 2 tablespoons (30 mL) lime juice
- 400 mL (14 oz) can full-fat coconut milk, stirred
- ¼ cup (60 mL) fresh Thai basil leaves (omit if you can't source)

Note: It's important not to jar this soup under pressure because of how thick it is.

INSTRUCTIONS

1. Brush the squash with about 2 tablespoons (30 mL) of olive oil and then sprinkle the finishing salt on top.

2. Place the squash on the air fryer oven racks. Place the racks in the oven.

3. Using the Air Fry function, set to 375°F (190°C) for 15 minutes. Rotate the trays when the Rotate Food alarm sounds. You want the squash to be slightly caramelized. **Note:** If you don't have an oven-style air fryer, you can do this in batches in a regular air fryer; you'll need to add 3–5 minutes to the cook time. You can also use a regular oven, 30 minutes on the middle rack.

4. Remove the squash from the air fryer and let it sit until cool to the touch.

5. Spoon the meat of the squash into a large bowl. If well done, the skin will peel off easily. Set aside.

6. Turn the electric pressure cooker on to Sauté.

7. Once it's hot, add the remaining 1 tablespoon (15 mL) of olive oil, the Ginger-Garlic Masala, onions, and curry paste. Sauté until the onions are soft, 2–5 minutes. Press Cancel.

8. Add the broth, fish sauce, brown sugar, lime juice, and cooked squash to the pressure cooker.

9. Place and seal the lid. Set to High Pressure for 5 minutes.

10. Natural-release pressure for 10 minutes, then quick-release any remaining pressure.

11. Remove the lid. Add the coconut milk. Blend well with the immersion blender. If you are using a heat-safe blender, add the contents of the pressure cooker and the coconut milk to the blender. Use the Purée or Smoothie setting to blend well.

12. Add the Thai basil to taste when serving.

Nutrition Facts

Thai Winter Squash Soup
Per 1 ½ cups (375 mL)

Calories 344

Calories from fat 225

% Daily Value*

Fat 25 g	38%
Saturated 16 g	100%
Polyunsaturated 1 g	
Monounsaturated 7 g	
Sodium 1,188 mg	52%
Potassium 848 mg	24%
Carbohydrate 30 g	10%
Fibre 5 g	21%
Sugars 9 g	10%
Protein 6 g	12%
Vitamin A 345 iu	71%
Vitamin C 25 mg	30%
Calcium 103 mg	10%
Iron 4 mg	22%

*Percent Daily Values are based on a 2,000-calorie diet.

BREAD MACHINE AND
AIR FRYER PACZKI

Paczki is the ultimate jelly doughnut. That is the bias of my Polish heritage talking. The first recorded recipe for a jelly doughnut is Polish in origin. Throughout the last 600 years, jelly- and custard-filled doughnuts have become an important part of many cultures. And it isn't coincidental that they are a staple during Hanukkah. The Polish variety of paczki with which I grew up is very much like the sufganiyot served during Hanukkah. If your jelly doughnut has icing sugar on it, chances are there is an unnamed Polish Jew behind its history.

While this air fryer adaptation forgoes the deep-frying that is an import part of both Polish and Jewish tradition, it isn't an attempt to make a healthier version, which seems to be the trend these days. The reason, as with every recipe in this book, has to do with keeping such an important staple accessible for those with disabilities.

Bread Machine and Air Fryer Paczki

If you need to brush it with extra oil before air frying to satisfy that cultural need, please do! The important thing about my adaptation is that it lessens the danger inherent in deep-frying doughnuts when disabled: the increased burn risk that arises because of mobility issues and/or executive function impairments.

PREP:	OVEN-STYLE AIR FRYER:	COMBO-STYLE AIR FRYER:	TOTAL:
10 minutes + rising time	6–10 minutes	20–24 minutes	16–34 minutes + rising time

CUISINE:	STORAGE:	SERVINGS:	CALORIES PER SERVING:
Polish	Eat within 3 days or freeze	12 doughnuts	207 kcal

Gather Equipment:

- 1½ or 2 lb (680 or 900 g) bread machine
- Measuring cups and spoons
- Dough cutter
- Oven-style air fryer or 8-quart (7.57 L) electric pressure cooker–air fryer combo
- Trivet and the bottom of a springform pan if using a combo-style air fryer
- Cooling rack
- Pastry brush
- Medium freezer bag
- Icing piper with long nozzle with wide opening

Prepare and Mise en Place Ingredients:

- ⅔ cup (160 mL) milk
- ¼ cup (60 mL) sugar
- 3 tablespoons (45 mL) vegetable oil
- 2 egg yolks
- ½ teaspoon (2.5 mL) vanilla extract
- 1¾ cups (415 mL) all-purpose flour (plus flour for rolling)
- ¼ teaspoon (1.25 mL) salt
- 2 teaspoons (10 mL) instant yeast
- 1 tablespoon (15 mL) melted unsalted butter

- ⅓ cup (80 mL) icing sugar, in the freezer bag
- 1 cup (250 mL) strawberry jam (or your jam, custard, or filling of choice)

Tip: If you don't have icing bags, you can cut a slit into the side of each doughnut and fill it using a small spoon. Note that if you let the doughnuts sit for any amount of time or freeze them, the icing sugar will form a glaze and they will no longer be powdered doughnuts.

INSTRUCTIONS

1. Add the milk, sugar, oil, egg yolks, and vanilla extract to the bread machine.
2. Add the flour and salt on top of the wet ingredients.
3. Make a dent in the flour and add the yeast in the dent.
4. Program the bread machine for the Dough cycle. Press Start.
5. Let it do its thing, including leaving it for the entire rise time.
6. Once the dough is ready, on a floured surface, gently roll the dough into a log about 7.5 cm (3 inches) in diameter. Be careful not to overly deflate the dough.
7. Cut the log into 12 pieces of equal size.

If using an oven-style air fryer:

1. Using the Bake setting, set to 375°F (190°C) for 5 minutes. Let the oven preheat.
2. Place 6 doughnuts per tray.
3. When the Add Food indicator goes off, place one tray with doughnuts on the bottom rung of the oven.
4. Cook for 3–5 minutes, until golden brown.
5. Remove the cooked doughnuts and place them on a cooling rack.
6. Repeat steps 1–5.

If using an electric pressure cooker–air fryer combo:

1. Put the bottom of a springform pan on a trivet in the bottom of the inner pot. Place 6 doughnuts on the pan.
2. Place the air frying lid.
3. Using the Bake setting, air fry at 375°F (190°C) for 10–12 minutes, until golden brown.
4. Remove the cooked doughnuts and place them on a cooling rack.
5. Repeat steps 1–4.

To powder and finish the doughnuts:

1. Brush the doughnuts with the melted butter.
2. In the freezer bag containing the icing sugar, roll each buttered doughnut to cover it with sugar. Place each powdered doughnut on the cooling rack.
3. Prepare the icing bag by affixing the nozzle. Place the jam (or filling of choice) in the icing bag.
4. Push the nozzle into the side of a doughnut. Squeeze the jam into the doughnut. The jam will start seeping out of the doughnut when it's filled. Repeat until all the doughnuts are filled.

Nutrition Facts

Paczki
Per 1 doughnut

Calories 207

Calories from fat 27

	% Daily Value*
Fat 3 g	5%
Saturated 1 g	6%
Trans 1 g	
Polyunsaturated 1 g	
Monounsaturated 1 g	
Cholesterol 36 mg	12%
Sodium 66 mg	3%
Potassium 82 mg	2%
Carbohydrate 43 g	14%
Fibre 1 g	4%
Sugars 22 g	24%
Protein 4 g	8%
Vitamin A 94 iu	2%
Vitamin C 2 mg	2%
Calcium 29 mg	3%
Iron 1 mg	6%

*Percent Daily Values are based on a 2,000-calorie diet.

Bread Machine Instant Potato Bread

Potato bread is one of my favourite white breads. It has a long history in eastern European cuisines, with speculation that it originated in Poland. Versions of it are also staples in some Jewish diets in Germany. The problem with potato bread is that you need to either make mashed potatoes first or have leftovers. In my house, leftover mashed potatoes are a rarity. And even though it takes little effort to do potatoes in an electric pressure cooker, bread takes three hours to make, and I just want to dump things and walk away without the added time of the pressure cooker. That's why I use instant mashed potato flakes.

This bread is perfect to serve with chili, spaghetti, soups, and stew.

PREP:	COOK:	TOTAL:	
5 minutes	3 hours	3 hours, 5 minutes	
CUISINE:	**STORAGE:**	**SERVINGS:**	**CALORIES PER SERVING:**
Eastern European	Eat within 3 days or freeze	12 slices in a 1½ lb (680 g) loaf; 16 slices in a 2 lb (900 g) loaf	141 kcal

Gather Equipment:

- 1½ or 2 lb (680 or 900 g) bread machine
- Measuring cups and spoons
- Cooling rack

Prepare and Mise en Place Ingredients:

For a 1.5 lb (680 g) loaf:

- ⅔ cup (160 mL) buttermilk
- ½ cup (120 mL) water
- 1½ tablespoons (22.5 mL) extra-virgin olive oil
- 1½ tablespoons (22.5 mL) liquid honey
- 2½ cups (592 mL) bread flour
- ½ cup (120 mL) instant mashed potato flakes
- 1 tablespoon (15 mL) vital wheat gluten
- 1½ teaspoons (7.5 mL) salt
- 1¼ teaspoons (6.25 mL) instant yeast or 2¼ teaspoons (11.25 mL) bread machine yeast

For a 2 lb (900 g) loaf:

- ¾ cup (180 mL) buttermilk
- ¾ cup (180 mL) water
- 2 tablespoons (30 mL) extra-virgin olive oil
- 2 tablespoons (30 mL) liquid honey
- 3 cups (708 mL) bread flour
- ½ cup (120 mL) instant mashed potato flakes
- 1 tablespoon plus 1 teaspoon (20 mL) vital wheat gluten
- 1½ teaspoons (7.5 mL) salt
- 2 teaspoons (10 mL) instant yeast or 2½ teaspoons (12.5 mL) bread machine yeast

INSTRUCTIONS

1. Add the buttermilk, water, olive oil, and honey to the bread machine.

2. In the following order, add the flour, instant mashed potato flakes, vital wheat gluten, and salt on top of the wet ingredients. It's important to make sure the potato flakes don't touch the liquid or they'll begin to absorb the liquid too soon.

3. Make a dent in the dry ingredients and add the yeast in the dent.

4. Set the crust to medium and program the bread machine for the Basic cycle. Press Start. **Note:** This recipe is not suitable for delayed cooking because of the risk of the potato flakes absorbing the liquids and the milk going bad.

5. When it's done, immediately remove the bread from the machine and let it cool on a cooling rack.

Nutrition Facts

Instant Potato Bread
Per 1 slice

Calories 141

Calories from fat 27

% Daily Value*

Fat 3 g	5%
Saturated 1 g	6%
Polyunsaturated 1 g	
Monounsaturated 1 g	
Cholesterol 1 mg	0%
Sodium 309 mg	13%
Potassium 86 mg	2%
Carbohydrate 24 g	8%
Fibre 1 g	4%
Sugars 3 g	3%
Protein 5 g	10%
Vitamin A 23 iu	0%
Vitamin C 2 mg	2%
Calcium 22 mg	2%
Iron 1 mg	6%

*Percent Daily Values are based on a 2,000-calorie diet.

Bread Machine Cornbread

One of the things I love about bread machines, aside from the fact they make it incredibly easy to make bread, is that they also do cakes. Cornbread is technically a cake because of the ingredients used. I love cornbread for its versatility. Not only is it great with butter for serving with chili, soups, and stews, but it's also great served warm with melted butter and maple syrup as a dessert.

PREP: 5 minutes	**COOK:** 1 hour, 40 minutes	**TOTAL:** 1 hour, 45 minutes
CUISINE: American	**STORAGE:** Eat within 3 days or freeze	**SERVINGS:** 16 squares	**CALORIES PER SERVING:** 150 kcal

Gather Equipment:

- 1½ or 2 lb (680 or 900 g) bread machine
- Measuring cups and spoons
- Cooling rack

Prepare and Mise en Place Ingredients:

- 1 large egg
- 1½ cups (356 mL) buttermilk
- ¼ cup plus 2 tablespoons (90 mL) melted unsalted butter
- ½ cup (120 mL) sugar
- 1 cup (236 mL) fine- or medium-grind yellow cornmeal
- 1 cup (236 mL) unbleached all-purpose flour
- 2 tablespoons (30 mL) roasted wheat germ
- 1 teaspoon (5 mL) baking soda
- ½ teaspoon (2.5 mL) baking powder
- ½ teaspoon (2.5 mL) salt

INSTRUCTIONS

1. Add the egg, buttermilk, melted butter, and sugar to the bread machine in the order listed.
2. In the following order, add the cornmeal, flour, wheat germ, baking soda, baking powder, and salt on top of the wet ingredients.
3. Set the crust to medium and program the bread machine for the Quick Bread/Cake cycle. Press Start. **Note:** This recipe is not suitable for delayed cooking because of the egg.
4. When it's done, let it sit in the pan for 10–15 minutes until the sides contract away from the pan.
5. Remove the cornbread and set it on a cooling rack.

Nutrition Facts
Cornbread
Per 1 square

Calories 150

Calories from fat 54	
% Daily Value*	
Fat 6 g	9%
Saturated 3 g	19%
Trans 1 g	
Polyunsaturated 1 g	
Monounsaturated 2 g	
Cholesterol 25 mg	8%
Sodium 184 mg	8%
Potassium 83 mg	2%
Carbohydrate 21 g	7%
Fibre 1 g	4%
Sugars 8 g	9%
Protein 3 g	6%
Vitamin A 187 iu	4%
Calcium 38 mg	4%
Iron 1 mg	6%

*Percent Daily Values are based on a 2,000-calorie diet.

Bread Machine Orange Cinnamon Loaf

There are few things I love more than a good dessert loaf. They are so versatile. Have a slice for breakfast with some fruit and cream cheese. Or as part of afternoon tea. Or, as the name implies, for dessert. I developed this recipe when I was craving the flavours of Christmas but didn't want something that felt seasonal.

PREP:	COOK:	TOTAL:
10 minutes	1 hour, 40 minutes	1 hour, 50 minutes

CUISINE:	STORAGE:	SERVINGS:	CALORIES PER SERVING:
Northern European	Eat within 3 days or freeze	16 slices	127 kcal

Gather Equipment:

- 1½ or 2 lb (680 or 900 g) bread machine
- Measuring cups and spoons
- Zester or small-hole grater
- Cooling rack

Prepare and Mise en Place Ingredients:

- ⅔ cup (160 mL) water
- ½ cup (120 mL) orange juice
- 1 large egg, room temperature
- 2 tablespoons (30 mL) unsalted butter, melted
- 1 teaspoon (5 mL) vanilla extract
- 1 cup (236 mL) sugar
- 2 cups (472 mL) all-purpose flour
- 1 teaspoon (5 mL) ground cinnamon
- 1 teaspoon (5 mL) baking powder
- ½ teaspoon (2.5 mL) baking soda
- ¼ teaspoon (1.25 mL) salt
- 1 tablespoon (15 mL) orange zest (from approx 1 navel orange)

INSTRUCTIONS

1. In the following order, add the water, orange juice, egg, melted butter, vanilla extract, and sugar to the bread machine.

2. In the order listed, add the flour, cinnamon, baking powder, baking soda, salt, and orange zest on top of the wet ingredients.

3. Set the crust to medium and program the bread machine for the Quick Bread/Cake cycle. Press Start. **Note:** This recipe is not suitable for delayed cooking because of the egg.

4. When it's done, let it sit in the pan for 10–15 minutes until the sides contract away from the pan.

5. Remove the loaf and set it on a cooling rack.

Bread Machine Lemon Pound Cake

Pound cake is one of the oldest northern European desserts in any recipe book. I like to use full-fat Greek yogourt to give my cakes that extra something.

PREP:	COOK:	TOTAL:	
10 minutes	1 hour, 40 minutes	1 hour, 50 minutes	
CUISINE:	**STORAGE:**	**SERVINGS:**	**CALORIES PER**
Northern European	Eat within 3 days or freeze	16 slices	**SERVING:** 214 kcal

Gather Equipment:

- 1½ or 2 lb (680 or 900 g) bread machine
- Measuring cups and spoons
- Zester or small-hole grater
- Cooling rack

Prepare and Mise en Place Ingredients:

- 1 cup (236 mL) unsalted butter, melted
- 4 large eggs, room temperature
- 2 tablespoons (30 mL) full-fat Greek yogourt
- 2 tablespoons (30 mL) 2 percent milk
- 2 tablespoons (30 mL) lemon juice
- 1 teaspoon (5 mL) vanilla extract
- 1 cup (236 mL) sugar
- 1½ cups (354 mL) all-purpose flour
- 1 teaspoon (5 mL) baking powder
- ½ teaspoon (2.5 mL) salt
- ¼ teaspoon (1.25 mL) baking soda
- 1 tablespoon (15 mL) lemon zest (from approx 2 lemons)

INSTRUCTIONS

1. In the following order, add the melted butter, eggs, yogourt, milk, lemon juice, vanilla extract, and sugar to the bread machine.
2. In the order listed, add the flour, baking powder, salt, baking soda, and lemon zest on top of the wet ingredients.
3. Set the crust to medium and program the bread machine for the Quick Bread/Cake cycle. Press Start. **Note:** This recipe is not suitable for delayed cooking because of the egg and milk.
4. When it's done, let it sit in the pan for 10–15 minutes until the sides contract away from the pan.
5. Remove the pound cake and set it on a cooling rack.

Nutrition Facts

Lemon Pound Cake
Per 1 slice

Calories 214

Calories from fat 117

% Daily Value*

Fat 13 g		20%
Saturated 8 g		50%
Trans 1 g		
Polyunsaturated 1 g		
Monounsaturated 3 g		
Cholesterol 77 mg		26%
Sodium 138 mg		6%
Potassium 42 mg		1%
Carbohydrate 22 g		7%
Fibre 1 g		4%
Sugars 13 g		14%
Protein 3 g		6%
Vitamin A 424 iu		8%
Vitamin C 1 mg		1%
Calcium 32 mg		3%
Iron 1 mg		6%

*Percent Daily Values are based on a 2,000-calorie diet.

Bread Machine Roti

While you'll still need a stovetop-like cooking surface to cook the roti, I've included this recipe to teach you how to use your bread machine to mix doughs if you have hand-related disabilities and can't afford a stand mixer to do the job. You could cook the roti in an air fryer, similar to the method in the Matzo Meal recipe (page 60), but it changes the flavour that is the result of direct heat from quickly frying it on a really hot pan and then puffing it up over hot air. Cooking it in the air fryer is also tricky because it can go from a pliable flatbread to a cracker in a second. The ability to feel the texture of the roti is an important part of the cooking process.

PREP: 20 minutes	**COOK:** 28 minutes	**TOTAL:** 48 minutes
CUISINE: Indian	**STORAGE:** Eat within 1 week or freeze	**SERVINGS:** 14	**CALORIES PER SERVING:** 70 kcal

Gather Equipment:

- Bread machine
- Measuring cups and spoons
- Pasta roller or French rolling pin
- Cooktop
- Griddle or frying pan
- Trivet (optional)
- Pastry brush

Mise en Place Ingredients:

- 1 cup (236 mL) whole wheat flour
- 1 cup (236 mL) all-purpose flour
- 1 tablespoon (15 mL) salt
- 1 tablespoon extra-virgin olive oil
- ⅔ cup plus 1 tablespoon (175 mL) warm water
- Melted butter or ghee as needed

INSTRUCTIONS

1. Put both types of flour and the salt, olive oil, and water in the bread machine.
2. Turn on to the Dough setting and let it mix until it's a round, smooth ball of dough, about 10 minutes.
3. Press Cancel/Stop. Let the dough sit for 10 minutes to allow the glutens to break down.
4. Separate into 14 round balls about 2.5 cm (1 inch) in diameter.
5. Flatten the balls slightly with the palms of your hands. Run through the pasta roller at setting 8.
6. Rotate the flattened dough 90 degrees and then run through the pasta roller at setting 4. If you are using a rolling pin, roll until about 2.5 mm (1/10 inch) thick.
7. Repeat until all the roti are rolled.
8. Heat a griddle or frying pan on medium-high heat. Once it's hot, dry fry each roti for 1–2 minutes per side, just long enough for a few browned spots to form.

(continued on next page)

9. If using a non-induction cooktop, place a trivet over an element on high heat. After each roti is done frying, place the roti over the trivet. The roti should start to puff up with the hot air coming from the element. If it doesn't start to puff up, remove it from the trivet before the roti begins to burn or becomes stiff. Skip this step if the roti puffed during step 8 or if you have an induction cooktop.

10. Brush each roti with melted butter or ghee.

11. Serve with your favourite spicy food.

Nutrition Facts

Roti
Per 1 roti (without butter/ghee)

Calories 70

Calories from fat 9

% Daily Value*

Fat 1 g	2%
Saturated 1 g	6%
Polyunsaturated 1 g	
Monounsaturated 1 g	
Sodium 499 mg	22%
Potassium 41 mg	1%
Carbohydrate 13 g	4%
Fibre 1 g	4%
Sugars 1 g	1%
Protein 2 g	4%
Vitamin A 1 iu	0%
Calcium 5 mg	1%
Iron 1 mg	6%

*Percent Daily Values are based on a 2,000-calorie diet.

SOME EFFORT

MEDIUM PREP TIMES

Electric Pressure Cooker Refried Beans

It is a common misconception that refried beans are a long-time traditional staple of Mexican cuisine. The reality is this dish is relatively new and tends to be confined to northern Mexico. It is simplistic in ingredients and versatile. You can use many types of fat: bacon grease, lard, duck fat, butter, or oil. To give mine a little something extra, I like to prepare it with bacon. I don't do this often because pork doesn't agree with me, but sometimes I crave that smoked flavour.

While this recipe takes little time to prepare, it's included in this section of the cookbook because the needed time at the end to fry the bean paste does take up a fair number of "spoons."

PREP:	COOK:	NATURAL RELEASE:	TOTAL:
10 minutes	1 hour, 10 minutes	10 minutes	1 hour, 30 minutes

CUISINE:	HEAT INDEX:	STORAGE:	SERVINGS:	CALORIES PER SERVING:
Mexican/Tex-Mex	Mild	Eat within 3 days or freeze	5 × ¾ cup (185 mL)	491 kcal

Gather Equipment:

- 6-quart (5.68 L) electric pressure cooker
- Cutting board
- Knife
- Measuring cups and spoons
- Fine-mesh strainer
- Heat-proof glass measuring cup
- Potato masher
- Can opener
- Wooden spoon

Prepare and Mise en Place Ingredients:

- 375 g (13 oz) package low-sodium bacon
- 1 medium yellow onion, diced
- 6 cloves garlic, sliced lengthwise
- 2 teaspoons (10 mL) ground cumin
- 1 teaspoon (5 mL) salt
- 1 cup (250 mL) dried pinto beans
- 3 cups (750 mL) water
- 156 mL (5.5 oz) can tomato paste
- 1 tablespoon (15 mL) lemon juice
- 1 teaspoon (5 mL) ground cayenne pepper

Substitution: To make this recipe vegetarian, omit the bacon and instead add 3 tablespoons (45 mL) of your fat of choice and 1 teaspoon (5 mL) liquid smoke or smoked paprika during the frying step.

INSTRUCTIONS

1. Turn your electric pressure cooker on to Sauté. Add the bacon. Sauté for 5–7 minutes until the bacon is thoroughly cooked. *Do not cook until crispy.* You want to cook it long enough for all the fat and water to separate from the bacon. **Note:** Typically, bacon would be removed here. However, if you want extra protein and flavour, keep the bacon. It will almost melt during the pressure cook phase and easily mash up with the beans. The calorie information for this recipe includes the bacon.

2. Add the onions, garlic, cumin, and salt. Sauté until the onions are translucent, about 2–3 minutes.

3. Press Cancel. Add the beans and water.

4. Place and seal the lid. Cook at High Pressure for 40 minutes.

5. Natural-release pressure for 10 minutes, then quick-release any remaining pressure.

6. Drain the bean-and-bacon mixture using a fine-mesh strainer, reserving the liquid in a glass measuring cup.

7. Place the inner pot back into the electric pressure cooker. Put the drained bean mixture back into the inner pot.

8. Turn the electric pressure cooker on to Sauté.

9. While it's warming up, mash the bean mixture.

10. Add the tomato paste, lemon juice, and cayenne pepper.

11. While stirring constantly, fry the beans for 10–15 minutes, adding a little bit of the reserved liquid to deglaze the inner pot as needed. Press Cancel when it's the desired consistency. This is a matter of personal preference.

12. Serve with rice, in a burrito or taco, or with your favourite Tex-Mex meal.

Nutrition Facts

Refried Beans
Per ¾ cup (185 mL)

Calories 491

Calories from fat 279

% Daily Value*

Fat 31 g	48%
Saturated 10 g	63%
Trans 1 g	
Polyunsaturated 5 g	
Monounsaturated 13 g	
Cholesterol 50 mg	17%
Sodium 1,223 mg	53%
Potassium 1,075 mg	31%
Carbohydrate 35 g	12%
Fibre 8 g	33%
Sugars 6 g	7%
Protein 20 g	40%
Vitamin A 681 iu	14%
Vitamin C 14 mg	17%
Calcium 83 mg	8%
Iron 4 mg	22%

*Percent Daily Values are based on a 2,000-calorie diet.

Electric Pressure Cooker
Thai Red Curry with Chicken

Proper Thai flavouring is so difficult to achieve in the electric pressure cooker. It's amazing how different cooking heat sources change the flavour. While authentic Thai recipes are *so hard* to create for the electric pressure cooker, the results are well worth it. This authentic Thai dish is a great balance of sweet and spicy. This recipe is much milder than a typical Thai red curry. Increase the amount of curry paste to six tablespoons (90 mL) for full flavour.

PREP:	COOK:	NATURAL RELEASE:	TOTAL:	
20 minutes	9 minutes	10 minutes	39 minutes	
CUISINE:	HEAT INDEX:	STORAGE:	SERVINGS:	CALORIES PER SERVING:
Thai	Mild	Freeze, or jar the curry at 11 lb (76 kPa) of pressure for 75 minutes and freeze the rice	4 × 2 cups (500 mL) with 1 cup (250 mL) rice	807 kcal

Gather Equipment:

- 6-quart (5.68 L) electric pressure cooker
- Cutting board
- Knife
- Food processor (or a cheese grater to shred the carrot)
- Wooden spoon
- Can opener
- 3-quart (2.84 L) electric pressure cooker

Prepare and Mise en Place Ingredients:

- 1½ tablespoons (22.5 mL) coconut oil
- 2½ tablespoons (37.5 mL) Thai red curry paste (approx)
- 4 dehydrated whole red chilies (approx)
- ½ cup (125 mL) no-salt-added chicken broth
- 1 chicken bouillon cube
- 1 carrot, shredded
- 5 large cherry tomatoes, cut in half
- 2 orange bell peppers, diced or cut in bite-sized pieces
- 1 medium yellow onion, diced or chopped
- 1 Thai eggplant, diced or cut in bite-sized pieces
- 1 tablespoon (15 mL) brown sugar
- ½ tablespoon (7.5 mL) lime juice (or lemon juice)
- ½ teaspoon (2.5 mL) dried basil
- 4 fresh Thai basil leaves (omit if you can't source)
- 454 g (1 lb) boneless skinless chicken thighs, cubed
- ½ teaspoon (2.5 mL) fish sauce
- 400 mL (14 oz) can full-fat coconut milk, stirred

For the rice:
- 2 cups (500 mL) jasmine rice, rinsed
- 2 cups (500 mL) water
- 1 teaspoon (5 mL) coconut oil

Note: If using two inner pots, the cook time and the natural release time will each increase by 10 minutes.

If canning, *do not* jar the curry with the rice, or it will lose its heat. Freeze the rice if you are jarring the curry.

Substitution: To make this dish vegetarian, substitute ¾ cup (185 mL) cashews for the chicken and ½ cup (125 mL) no-salt-added vegetable broth for the chicken broth. The time under pressure remains the same. Adjust the amount of curry paste and/or chilies according to your heat preference. If you can't get Thai eggplant, you can substitute a small Italian eggplant, Japanese eggplant, or zucchini. Omit the fresh Thai basil if you can't get it.

INSTRUCTIONS

1. Turn the 6-quart electric pressure cooker on to Sauté. When it's hot, add the coconut oil, curry paste, and dehydrated chilies. Sauté for a couple of minutes.
2. Add the chicken broth and bouillon cube. Sauté until the bouillon cube has mostly dissolved. Press Cancel.
3. Add the carrot, cherry tomatoes, bell peppers, onions, and eggplant. Add the brown sugar, lime juice, dried basil, and fresh Thai basil. Add the chicken. Sprinkle the chicken with the fish sauce.
4. Place and seal the lid. Cook at High Pressure for 5 minutes.
5. Natural-release pressure for 10 minutes, then quick-release any remaining pressure.
6. Remove the lid. Turn on to Sauté. Stir in the coconut milk. Let it boil for a couple of minutes. Serve with jasmine rice.

For the rice:

1. While the curry is cooking, in a 3-quart (2.84 L) electric pressure cooker, add the rice, water, and coconut oil.
2. Place and seal the lid. Cook at High Pressure for 4 minutes.
3. Naturally release pressure for 10 minutes, then quick-release any remaining pressure. Makes four 1-cup (250 mL) servings.

Nutrition Facts

Thai Red Curry
with Chicken
Per 2 cups (500 mL) + 1
cup (250 mL) rice

Calories 807

Calories from fat 297

% Daily Value*

Fat 33 g	51%
Saturated 25 g	156%
Cholesterol 108 mg	36%
Sodium 449 mg	20%
Potassium 1,058 mg	30%
Carbohydrate 95 g	32%
Fibre 6 g	25%
Sugars 12 g	13%
Protein 33 g	66%
Vitamin A 6,762 iu	135%
Vitamin C 118 mg	143%
Calcium 95 mg	10%
Iron 6 mg	33%

*Percent Daily Values are based on a 2,000-calorie diet.

Electric Pressure Cooker Middle Eastern–Inspired Rice Bowl

This dish is quick and relatively easy to make. Rice bowls are common throughout the Middle East. They may seem simple but the way tangy, sour, and sweet are combined in Middle Eastern cuisine causes an explosion of flavour in your mouth. Also, they are a great balanced meal in one bowl.

PREP:	COOK:	NATURAL RELEASE:	TOTAL:	
20 minutes	6 minutes	10 minutes	36 minutes	

CUISINE:	HEAT INDEX:	STORAGE:	SERVINGS:	CALORIES PER SERVING:
Middle Eastern	Mild	Refrigerate for up to 3 days	4	931 kcal

Gather Equipment:

- 3-quart (2.84 L) electric pressure cooker
- Cutting board
- Knife
- Measuring cups and spoons
- Fine-mesh strainer
- 3 small stainless steel mixing bowls
- Aluminum foil
- Trivet
- Non-stick flat pan or frying pan
- Tongs

Prepare and Mise en Place Ingredients:

- 1 red onion, thinly sliced
- 4 tablespoons (60 mL) red wine vinegar, divided in 2
- 2 teaspoons (10 mL) sugar
- 1 ½ cups (375 mL) basmati rice, rinsed
- 1 ½ cups (375 mL) water
- 1 teaspoon (5 mL) salt
- 1 teaspoon (5 mL) ghee
- 400 g (1 lb) halloumi cheese, rinsed, dried, and cut in 5 mm (¼-inch) slices
- 2 tablespoons (30 mL) harissa paste
- Ground cayenne pepper to taste (optional)
- ½ cup (125 mL) hummus (page 56)
- ¼ cup (60 mL) mayonnaise
- 1 teaspoon (5 mL) minced garlic
- 1 cup (250 mL) shredded red cabbage
- ½ cup (125 mL) julienned carrots
- 2 avocados, cut in bite-sized pieces

INSTRUCTIONS

1. In a small stainless steel mixing bowl, add the onion, 2 tablespoons of the vinegar, and the sugar. Cover with aluminum foil. Set aside.
2. In the electric pressure cooker, add the rice, water, salt, and ghee. Place the trivet on top of the rice. Place the bowl with the onions on top of the trivet.
3. Place and seal the lid. Cook at High Pressure for 4 minutes.
4. Natural-release pressure for 10 minutes, then quick-release any remaining pressure.
5. While the rice is cooking, preheat the non-stick pan. Once it's hot, fry the cheese until golden brown on each side, about 1–2 minutes per side.
6. Place the cheese in a bowl. Toss it with the harissa paste. Add cayenne pepper to taste if you don't find the harissa paste spicy enough. Set aside.
7. In a mixing bowl, whisk together the hummus, mayonnaise, remaining 2 tablespoons of vinegar, and garlic. Set aside.
8. Toss the cabbage with 1 tablespoon (15 mL) of the hummus sauce.
9. Once the rice and pickled onions are done, divide the rice among 4 serving dishes. Top with the divided carrots, avocados, cabbage, and pickled onions, and drizzle with the hummus sauce. Enjoy!

Nutrition Facts

Middle Eastern-Inspired
Rice Bowl
Per 1 bowl

Calories 931

Calories from fat 495

% Daily Value*	
Fat 55 g	85%
Saturated 22 g	138%
Cholesterol 9 mg	3%
Sodium 2,122 mg	92%
Potassium 810 mg	23%
Carbohydrate 79 g	26%
Fibre 11 g	46%
Sugars 7 g	8%
Protein 33 g	66%
Vitamin A 3,119 iu	62%
Vitamin C 27 mg	33%
Calcium 1,067 mg	107%
Iron 2 mg	11%

*Percent Daily Values are based on a 2,000-calorie diet.

Electric Pressure Cooker Mexican Ground Beef Casserole

When I was growing up, my first experience with Mexican food was TacoTime and Old El Paso taco kits. I loved the flavours, even if I didn't understand at the time that the things that appealed to me were the warm spices, the tang of citrus, and a little bit of sour. As I got older, Mexican food was still mainly the Canadian/American versions found in the homes of people who grew up on the fast-food offerings. Once I was able to go on my own food journey and learn more about the history of Mexican food—specifically Aztec and Maya food—interwoven with the history of colonization and how the food evolved, I became more interested in developing recipes that stayed true to those origins. I also wanted to make use of ingredients that became staples once South Asian spices were introduced when enslaved people's cuisine was woven into traditional dishes.

PREP:	COOK:	NATURAL RELEASE:	TOTAL:	
20 minutes	24 minutes	10 minutes	54 minutes	
CUISINE:	HEAT INDEX:	STORAGE:	SERVINGS:	CALORIES PER SERVING:
Mexican	Mild to medium	Freeze	8 × 1½ cups (375 mL)	389 kcal

Gather Equipment:

- 6-quart (5.68 L) electric pressure cooker
- Cutting board
- Knife
- Food processor or chopper attachment for the immersion blender
- Measuring cups and spoons
- Wooden spoon
- Can opener

Prepare and Mise en Place Ingredients:

- 454 g (1 lb) lean ground beef
- 2 medium yellow onions, diced or chopped
- ¼ cup (60 mL) water
- 2 large green bell peppers, diced or chopped
- 1 jalapeno pepper, diced or chopped (seed if too spicy, or add another for extra spice)
- 796 mL (28 oz) can no-salt-added diced tomatoes, with liquid
- 2 cups (500 mL) basmati rice, rinsed
- 2 tablespoons (30 mL) chili powder
- 1½ tablespoons (22.5 mL) salt
- 1 tablespoon (15 mL) ground cumin
- 1 tablespoon (15 mL) garlic powder
- 1 tablespoon (15 mL) paprika
- 2 teaspoons (10 mL) dried oregano
- 2 teaspoons (10 mL) onion powder
- 1 teaspoon (5 mL) black pepper
- 1 teaspoon (5 mL) red pepper flakes
- 796 mL (28 oz) can red kidney beans, drained and rinsed
- 1 cup (250 mL) water

Substitution: To make this dish vegetarian, replace the ground beef with the equivalent amount of your favourite ground plant-based product, like Impossible ground "beef." The time under pressure remains the same.

Tip: While this casserole is great on its own, you may serve it with sour cream, cheese, lime juice, avocado, lettuce, and sliced jalapenos, or mix it all together and wrap it in a burrito shell.

INSTRUCTIONS

1. Turn the electric pressure cooker on to Sauté. Once it's hot, add the ground beef and onions. Sauté until the ground beef is crumbly and the onions are translucent, about 2–4 minutes. Do not brown. Deglaze the pot with ¼ cup (60 mL) water.

2. Press Cancel. In even layers, add the following in the order listed: all peppers, diced tomatoes with liquid, rice, all the herbs and spices, and the kidney beans. Add 1 cup (250 mL) water.

3. Place and seal the lid. Cook at High Pressure for 20 minutes.

4. Natural-release pressure for 10 minutes, then quick-release any remaining pressure.

5. Remove the lid. Churn the casserole until well mixed. Serve. Enjoy!

Nutrition Facts

Mexican Ground Beef Casserole
Per 1 ½ cups (375 mL)

Calories 389

Calories from fat 45
% Daily Value*

Fat 5 g	8%
Saturated 2 g	13%
Cholesterol 35 mg	12%
Sodium 1,792 mg	78%
Potassium 920 mg	26%
Carbohydrate 65 g	22%
Fibre 10 g	42%
Sugars 7 g	8%
Protein 23 g	46%
Vitamin A 1,009 iu	20%
Vitamin C 47 mg	57%
Calcium 125 mg	13%
Iron 6 mg	33%

*Percent Daily Values are based on a 2,000-calorie diet.

Electric Pressure Cooker Hamburger Stew

I associate hamburger soup and stew with my church's monthly fellowship lunches and AGM lunches. It's also a food I appreciate for being nutrient dense at an exceptionally low cost. I grew up in the United Church of Canada. A church women's group—United Church Women, or UCW—would produce recipe books as a way for congregations across Canada to raise funds, since each congregation is responsible for paying all the costs associated with running it. People from congregations across Canada would submit their family's cornerstone recipe. These recipe books had a lot of recipes made popular on the prairies during the Dust Bowl and Great Depression. Every recipe book had multiple versions of hamburger soup and stew because they were low-cost dishes that sustained families through the difficult time in which they became popular.

My version of hamburger stew keeps this tradition. It's also easy to alter. Simply remove or add vegetables to your preference. The cook time will remain the same. You can easily turn it from a stew to a soup by not adding the cornstarch at the end.

PREP:	COOK:	NATURAL RELEASE:	TOTAL:	
20 minutes	10 minutes	10 minutes	40 minutes	
CUISINE:	**HEAT INDEX:**	**STORAGE:**	**SERVINGS:**	**CALORIES PER SERVING:**
Canadian	Mild	Freeze, or jar at 11 lb (76 kPa) of pressure for 75 minutes	9 × 2 cups (500 mL)	290 kcal

Gather Equipment:

- 6-quart (5.68 L) electric pressure cooker
- Cutting board
- Knife or food processor with dicing blade
- Measuring cups and spoons
- Wooden spoon
- Can opener

Prepare and Mise en Place Ingredients:

- 1 tablespoon (15 mL) extra-virgin olive oil
- 900 g (2 lb) lean ground beef
- 1 medium yellow onion, chopped
- 1 tablespoon (15 mL) minced garlic
- 4 cups (1 L) no-salt-added beef broth, divided in 2
- ¼ cup (60 mL) Worcestershire sauce
- 4 medium carrots, chopped
- 3 stalks celery, chopped
- 2 large russet potatoes, cubed
- 2 tablespoons (30 mL) Italian herb seasoning, paste or dried
- 2 teaspoons (10 mL) salt (or to taste)
- 2 teaspoons (10 mL) black pepper (or to taste)
- ½ teaspoon (2.5 mL) dried thyme
- ½ teaspoon (2.5 mL) dried parsley
- 1 bay leaf
- 796 mL (28 oz) can no-salt-added diced tomatoes, with liquid
- ¼ cup (60 mL) cornstarch
- ¼ cup (60 mL) cold water

Substitution: To make this dish vegetarian, replace the ground beef with the equivalent amount of your favourite ground plant-based product, like Impossible ground "beef," substitute no-salt-added vegetable broth for the beef broth, and omit the Worcestershire sauce. The time under pressure remains the same.

Variation: If you'd rather make hamburger soup, drain the beef after step 1 to remove some of the fat and do not add the cornstarch-and-water mixture at the end.

INSTRUCTIONS

1. Turn the electric pressure cooker on to Sauté. When it's hot, add the olive oil. When the oil takes on a shimmering, ripply appearance, add the ground beef, onions, and garlic. Lightly season with salt and pepper. Sauté until the ground beef is broken up, about 2–3 minutes. *Do not brown.*

2. Add 2 cups (500 mL) of the beef broth. Deglaze the pot. Press Cancel.

3. Add the Worcestershire sauce, carrots, celery, potatoes, Italian seasoning, salt, pepper, thyme, parsley, and bay leaf. Add the diced tomatoes on the top. Do not stir.

4. Place and seal the lid. Cook at High Pressure for 5 minutes.

5. Natural-release pressure for 10 minutes, then quick-release any remaining pressure.

6. Mix together the cornstarch and water.

7. Remove the lid. Turn on to Sauté. Add the remaining 2 cups (500 mL) of beef broth. Once it's boiling, add the cornstarch-and-water mixture and stir until thickened.

Nutrition Facts
Hamburger Stew
Per 2 cups (500 mL)

Calories 290

Calories from fat 63

% Daily Value*

Fat 7 g		11%
Saturated 3 g		19%
Cholesterol 63 mg		21%
Sodium 1,030 mg		45%
Potassium 1,257 mg		36%
Carbohydrate 30 g		10%
Fibre 4 g		17%
Sugars 6 g		7%
Protein 27 g		54%
Vitamin A 4,664 iu		93%
Vitamin C 17 mg		21%
Calcium 99 mg		10%
Iron 5 mg		28%

*Percent Daily Values are based on a 2,000-calorie diet.

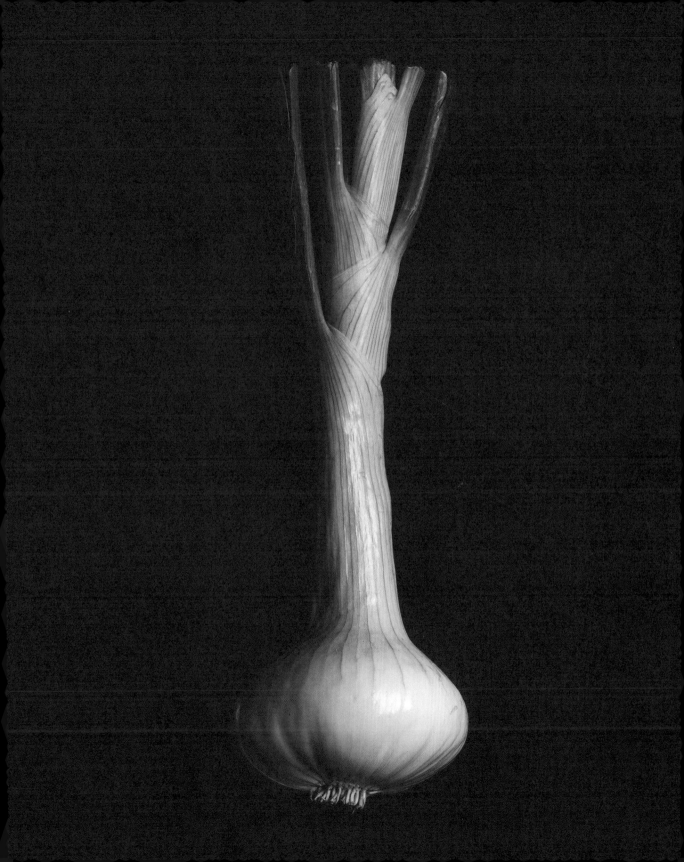

Electric Pressure Cooker Chicken Soup

Chicken soup. Nearly every type of cuisine has a version of chicken soup. Many years ago, I surprised myself when I first developed a chicken soup recipe. There was a time when I was convinced I hated soup that came from western European cuisine. Turned out, I hated canned soup, and that was all I was exposed to while I was growing up. In my early 20s I started to really experiment in the kitchen and turned away from following recipes. It was during this period of experimentation that I nailed a northern European–style of chicken soup that is great when you're feeling under the weather or simply need to be wrapped in a blanket of comfort.

PREP:	COOK:	NATURAL RELEASE:	TOTAL:	
25 minutes	1 hour, 2 minutes	20 minutes	1 hour, 47 minutes	
CUISINE:	**HEAT INDEX:**	**STORAGE:**	**SERVINGS:**	**CALORIES PER**
Northern European	Mild to medium	Freeze, or jar at 11 lb (76 kPa) of pressure for 75 minutes	6 × 2 cups (500 mL)	**SERVING:** 196 kcal

Gather Equipment:

- 6-quart (5.68 L) electric pressure cooker
- Cutting board
- Knife
- Food processor or chopper attachment for your immersion blender
- Vegetable peeler
- Garlic press and peeler
- Fine-hole grater
- Measuring cups and spoons
- Tongs
- Slotted ladle

Prepare and Mise en Place Ingredients:

- 1 chicken carcass from the Best Roast Chicken recipe (page 183), including the lemon, herbs, and garlic; or 1 kg (2 lb) chicken wings or 454 g (1 lb) boneless skinless chicken thighs
- 7 cups (1.75 L) water
- 4 large carrots, chopped
- 3 stalks celery, chopped in small pieces
- 1 large russet potato, cut in small cubes
- 1 medium onion, chopped
- 1 tablespoon (15 mL) minced garlic
- 1 tablespoon (15 mL) grated ginger
- 2 teaspoons (10 mL) salt
- 2 teaspoons (10 mL) black pepper
- 1 teaspoon (5 mL) dried parsley
- 1 teaspoon (5 mL) dried oregano
- 1 teaspoon (5 mL) dried rosemary
- 2 bay leaves

Substitution: To make this dish vegetarian, substitute one 796 mL (28 oz) can of chickpeas, drained, for the chicken. You can substitute 4 cups (1 L) frozen vegetables for the carrots and celery. If you think it will be too spicy for you, cut the ginger and pepper quantities in half.

INSTRUCTIONS

1. In a 6-quart (5.68 L) electric pressure cooker, add the leftover chicken carcass from your roast chicken—including the lemon, herbs and garlic—and the water. You can substitute chicken wings or boneless skinless chicken thighs for the carcass.

2. Place and seal the lid. Cook on the Soup/Broth setting for 1 hour. **Note:** If you use the Pressure setting, you will not get a clear broth.

3. Natural-release pressure for 10 minutes, then quick-release any remaining pressure.

4. Remove the lid. If you used bone-in chicken or a carcass to make the broth, using tongs and a slotted ladle, remove the chicken pieces and place them in a bowl. Separate the meat from the bones. Compost or discard the bones. If you used a carcass, also compost or discard the lemon peels and big chunks of herbs. Do your best to remove all the bones.

5. Dump the meat from step 4 and all the remaining ingredients into the electric pressure cooker.

6. Place and seal the lid. Cook at High Pressure for 2 minutes.

7. Natural-release pressure for 10 minutes, then quick-release any remaining pressure so as to not overcook the potato and veg.

Nutrition Facts

Chicken Soup
Per 2 cups (500 mL)

Calories 196

Calories from fat 54	
% Daily Value*	
Fat 6 g	9%
Saturated 1 g	6%
Polyunsaturated 2 g	
Monounsaturated 2 g	
Cholesterol 45 mg	15%
Sodium 1,146 mg	50%
Potassium 607 mg	17%
Carbohydrate 19 g	6%
Fibre 4 g	17%
Sugars 4 g	4%
Protein 17 g	34%
Vitamin A 9,000 iu	180%
Vitamin C 17.3 mg	21%
Calcium 70 mg	7%
Iron 1.8 mg	10%

*Percent Daily Values are based on a 2,000-calorie diet.

Electric Pressure Cooker Chicken Stew

By adding a thickening agent, such as cornstarch, chicken soup can easily be turned into a stew. This Chicken Stew recipe is included to demonstrate that, with just a few simple changes in ingredients, you can create a same-but-different dish that is more filling and has a heartier flavour profile.

PREP:	COOK:	NATURAL RELEASE:	TOTAL:	
20 minutes	9 minutes	10 minutes	39 minutes	
CUISINE:	HEAT INDEX:	STORAGE:	SERVINGS:	CALORIES PER SERVING:
Northern European	Mild	Freeze, or jar at 11 lb (76 kPa) of pressure for 75 minutes	8 × 2 cups (500 mL)	300 kcal

Gather Equipment:

- 6-quart (5.68 L) electric pressure cooker
- Cutting board
- Knife
- Garlic press
- Food processor or food chopper attachment for your immersion blender
- Measuring cups and spoons
- Wooden spoo
- Small bowl or glass

Prepare and Mise en Place Ingredients:

- 2 tablespoons (30 mL) extra-virgin olive oil
- 1 medium yellow onion, chopped
- 6 cloves garlic, minced or pressed
- 4 cups (1 L) no-salt-added chicken broth
- 4 large carrots, chopped
- 2 large russet potatoes, cut in medium-sized cubes
- 4 stalks celery, chopped
- 2 cups (500 mL) frozen green beans
- 1 teaspoon (5 mL) ground sage
- 1 teaspoon (5 mL) dried rosemary
- 1 teaspoon (5 mL) dried parsley
- 1 teaspoon (5 mL) dried basil
- 1 teaspoon (5 mL) salt
- 1 teaspoon (5 mL) black pepper
- 454 g (1 lb) boneless skinless chicken thighs, cubed
- 6 tablespoons (90 mL) cornstarch
- 1 cup (250 mL) water

Substitution: To make this dish vegetarian, substitute one 796 mL (28 oz) can of chickpeas, drained, for the chicken and no-salt-added vegetable broth for the chicken broth. Sometimes I replace the chicken broth with 2 cups (500 mL) frozen turkey drippings and 2 cups (500 mL) water.

Tip: Serve with grilled cheese or your favourite toasted sandwich.

INSTRUCTIONS

1. Turn the electric pressure cooker on to Sauté. Once it's hot, add the olive oil, onions, and garlic. Sauté until the onions are translucent, about 2 minutes. Do not brown. Press Cancel.

2. In the following order, add the chicken broth, carrots, potatoes, celery, frozen green beans, sage, rosemary, parsley, basil, salt, black pepper, and chicken.

3. Place and seal the lid. Cook at High Pressure for 5 minutes.

4. Natural-release pressure for 10 minutes, then quick-release any remaining pressure.

5. In the small bowl/glass mix together the cornstarch and water.

6. Remove the lid. Turn on to Sauté. Once the stew starts to boil, add the cornstarch-and-water mixture and stir until thickened. Press Cancel.

Nutrition Facts

Chicken Stew
Per 2 cups (500 mL)

Calories 300

Calories from fat 63	
% Daily Value*	
Fat 7 g	11%
Saturated 1 g	6%
Cholesterol 57 mg	19%
Sodium 566 mg	25%
Potassium 1,071 mg	31%
Carbohydrate 40 g	13%
Fibre 6 g	25%
Sugars 8 g	9%
Protein 18 g	36%
Vitamin A 7,095 iu	142%
Vitamin C 23.4 mg	28%
Calcium 91 mg	9%
Iron 2.9 mg	16%

*Percent Daily Values are based on a 2,000-calorie diet.

Electric Pressure Cooker Chicken Korma

Chicken korma is a dish that checks three boxes of Indian food preparation. It's a tikka. It's a curry. And it has a masala. *Korma* means to cook with coconut milk, ground nuts, and yogourt. Unlike butter chicken, korma has a long history in the Indian subcontinent, dating back at least 500 years. A lot of people associate it with Pakistan Panjab and Muslim holidays. That's why a lot of the recipes that are available use lamb or goat for the protein. But it's also very much a part of Indian Panjab and Sikh culture and has strong roots in Bangladesh as well. This dish became synonymous with these regions of the subcontinent when the Mughal Empire controlled the area.

PREP:	MARINATE:	COOK:	NATURAL RELEASE:	TOTAL:
20 minutes	2 hours (or up to overnight)	10 minutes	20 minutes	2 hours, 50 minutes

CUISINE:	HEAT INDEX:	STORAGE:	SERVINGS:	CALORIES PER SERVING:
Indian subcontinent	Mild to medium	Freeze, or jar at 11 lb (76 kPa) of pressure for 75 minutes	16 × 1 cup (250 mL) with 1 cup (250 mL) rice	630 kcal

Gather Equipment:

- Two 6-quart (5.68 L) electric pressure cookers, or one 6-quart (5.68 L) electric pressure cooker and a second inner pot
- Measuring cups and spoons
- Cutting board
- Knife
- Food processor or food chopper attachment for your immersion blender
- Stainless steel mixing bowl
- Can opener
- Blender
- Trivet
- Tongs
- Wooden spoon
- Aluminum foil

Prepare and Mise en Place Ingredients:

- ½ cup (60 mL) extra-virgin olive oil
- ¼ cup (60 mL) Ginger-Garlic Masala (page 44)
- 4 teaspoons (20 mL) Garam Masala (page 47)
- 4 teaspoons (20 mL) Thana Jeeroo (page 46)
- 3 teaspoons (15 mL) salt
- 2 teaspoons (10 mL) ground cayenne pepper
- 2 teaspoons (10 mL) ground turmeric
- 1.36 kg (3 lb) boneless skinless chicken thighs, cubed
- 2 cups (500 mL) full-fat plain Greek yogourt
- 398 mL (14 oz) can no-salt-added diced tomatoes, with liquid
- 2 medium yellow onions, chopped
- 1 cup (250 mL) raw almonds
- 1 cup (250 mL) water
- 400 mL (14 oz) can full-fat coconut milk, stirred
- 156 mL (5.5 oz) can tomato paste
- ¼ cup (60 mL) chopped cilantro
- 4 teaspoons (20 mL) brown sugar
- 2 teaspoons (10 mL) Garam Masala (page 47)

For the rice:
- 8 cups (2 L) basmati rice, rinsed
- 8 cups (2 L) water

Note: If using two inner pots, the cook time and the natural release time will each increase by 10 minutes.

Substitution: To make this vegetarian, substitute 3 cups (750 mL) cubed Paneer (page 59) for the chicken. Marinate it as you would the chicken. Change the time under pressure to 4 minutes.

INSTRUCTIONS

1. In a stainless steel mixing bowl, mix the olive oil, Ginger-Garlic Masala, first quantity of Garam Masala, Thana Jeeroo, salt, cayenne pepper, and turmeric to make a paste.
2. Add the chicken and thoroughly mix it with the spice paste.
3. Add the yogourt and mix well. Marinate for 2–4 hours in the fridge. You could even do this the night before.
4. In a blender, add the tomatoes, onions, almonds, and water. Blend into a smooth purée.
5. Pour the contents of the blender into a 6-quart (5.68 L) electric pressure cooker. Insert the trivet.
6. Pour the marinated chicken directly on top of the trivet.
7. Place and seal the lid. Cook at High Pressure for 5 minutes.
8. Natural-release pressure for 10 minutes, then quick-release any remaining pressure.
9. Remove the lid. Using tongs, remove the trivet, keeping the chicken in the pot. Stir in the coconut milk, tomato paste, cilantro, brown sugar, and second quantity of Garam Masala.
10. If using a second inner pot, remove the first inner pot containing the korma and set aside. Insert the second inner pot.

For the rice:

1. In the second inner pot—or, while the korma is cooking, in another 6-quart (5.68 L) electric pressure cooker—add the rice and water. You may want to line the pressure cooker with aluminum foil to prevent the burn warning from going off when cooking so much rice.
2. Place and seal the lid. Cook at High Pressure for 5 minutes.
3. Natural-release pressure for 10 minutes, then quick-release any remaining pressure.
4. Serve 1 cup (250 mL) korma with 1 cup (250 mL) rice.

Nutrition Facts

Chicken Korma
Per 1 cup (250 mL) + 1 cup (250 mL) rice

Calories 630

Calories from fat 162	
% Daily Value*	
Fat 18 g	28%
Saturated 7g	44%
Cholesterol 82 mg	27%
Sodium 653 mg	28%
Potassium 695 mg	20%
Carbohydrate 85 g	28%
Fibre 4 g	17%
Sugars 5 g	6%
Protein 29 g	58%
Vitamin A 305 iu	6%
Vitamin C 7.8 mg	9%
Calcium 123 mg	12%
Iron 3.2 mg	18%

*Percent Daily Values are based on a 2,000-calorie diet.

Electric Pressure Cooker Matzo Balls

This recipe and the Matzo Ball Soup recipe (page 211) are adaptations of a friend's traditional family recipe. It was important to me to adapt the recipe for the electric pressure cooker for a couple of reasons. The first has to do with my own Jewish ancestry. The second reason has to do with my Jewish friends who are also disabled. When one is disabled, being able to make matzo balls outside of Passover, without the need for the chicken fat and stock, is vital so they can be frozen, making the rest of the preparations more manageable. Also, they make for an excellent snack or addition to other soups.

PREP:	COOK:	NATURAL RELEASE:	TOTAL:
20 minutes + chilling time	17 minutes	10 minutes	47 minutes + chilling time

CUISINE:	HEAT INDEX:	STORAGE:	SERVINGS:	CALORIES PER SERVING:
Jewish kosher	None	Freeze	8 balls	110 kcal

Gather Equipment:

- 3-quart (2.84 L) electric pressure cooker
- Measuring cups and spoons
- Stainless steel mixing bowls
- Electric hand mixer or stand mixer
- Trivet
- Wooden spoon

Prepare and Mise en Place Ingredients:

- 4 large eggs
- 1 tablespoon (15 mL) dried dill or 2 tablespoons (30 mL) chopped fresh dill
- 1 tablespoon (15 mL) dried parsley or 2 tablespoons (30 mL) chopped fresh parsley
- 1 tablespoon (15 mL) unsalted butter, melted
- 1 teaspoon (5 mL) kosher salt
- ⅛ teaspoon (pinch) onion powder
- ¾ cup (185 mL) Matzo Meal (page 60)
- 2 cups (500 mL) chicken broth
- 2 cups (500 mL) water

INSTRUCTIONS

1. Chill a stainless steel mixing bowl.
2. Once the bowl is chilled, separate the eggs, placing the egg whites in the chilled bowl and the yolks in a separate bowl.
3. Using an electric hand mixer or stand mixer, beat the egg whites until they form stiff peaks. Put them in the fridge to chill until you need them.
4. In the bowl with the egg yolks, add the dill, parsley, melted butter, salt, and onion powder. Mix well.
5. Mix in the Matzo Meal a little at a time, until well combined.
6. Gradually fold in the egg whites, about a quarter of the egg whites at a time, until thoroughly mixed.
7. Cover and refrigerate for at least 1 hour. Refrigerate overnight to save "spoons."

8. Once the Matzo Ball mix has chilled, in a 3-quart (2.84 L) electric pressure cooker, add the chicken broth, the water, and the trivet. Turn on to Sauté. Heat until it boils, about 5 minutes.

9. While the stock is heating up, roll the Matzo Ball mix into 2 cm (¾-inch) balls.

10. Once the stock-and-water mixture is boiling, lightly drop the balls into the pot using a spoon. Make sure the balls are floating and not sticking to the trivet. The trivet is there just in case one falls apart, so it doesn't burn.

11. Press Cancel. Place and seal the lid. Set to High Pressure for 12 minutes.

12. Natural-release pressure for 10 minutes, then quick-release any remaining pressure.

13. Put the cooked Matzo Balls in a dish and set aside until ready to serve, or freeze them to use during Passover.

Nutrition Facts
Matzo Balls
Per ball

Calories 110

Calories from fat 45

% Daily Value*

Fat 5 g	8%
Saturated 2 g	13%
Cholesterol 89 mg	30%
Sodium 352 mg	15%
Potassium 63 mg	2%
Carbohydrate 11 g	4%
Fibre 0 g	0%
Sugars 0 g	0%
Protein 4 g	8%
Vitamin A 230 iu	5%
Vitamin C 0.4 mg	0%
Calcium 25 mg	3%
Iron 1 mg	6%

*Percent Daily Values are based on a 2,000-calorie diet.

ELECTRIC PRESSURE COOKER VIETNAMESE CHICKEN PHO

Pho is another dish with deep roots in colonialism, this time the French colonization of Vietnam. The dish originated sometime around the late 1800s. Before the French occupied Vietnam, beef was not a part of the diet. The French demanded it, so cows were slaughtered and for the first time beef became a part of Vietnamese cuisine. There is also a heavy influence from southern Chinese cuisine in this dish.

There have been many stories constructed around this dish. You may have read that pho tells the story of two lovers. Or you may have read that pho comes from the French pot-au-feu (pot on the fire). This story is based on the idea that "pho" and "feu" are pronounced nearly identically. In recent years, there has been pushback against these stories for being inaccurate. The pushback is in favour of highlighting pho's origins in the French occupation of Vietnam, as well as educating westerners about the rich history of Vietnamese cuisine predating colonization. Even though pho is the result of colonization, it is still very much loved and considered an important staple by many Vietnamese people.

I decided to include this recipe to highlight the rich mix of spices that have been used in the region for millennia and were once highly treasured during the days of Silk Road trading. Western food owes a lot to the rich food history of these areas, a history we, as colonizers, tried to erase and rewrite as inferior to the Western world.

Electric Pressure Cooker Vietnamese Chicken Pho

Instead of using beef, my Pho recipe uses a more traditional Vietnamese protein, chicken.

PREP:	**COOK:**	**NATURAL RELEASE:**	**TOTAL:**
20 minutes	1 hour, 10 minutes	10 minutes	1 hour, 40 minutes

CUISINE:	**HEAT INDEX:**	**STORAGE:**	**SERVINGS:**	**CALORIES PER SERVING:**
Vietnamese	Mild	Freeze, or jar at 11 lb (76 kPa) of pressure for 75 minutes (without the noodles)	4 × 2 cups (500 mL)	494 kcal

Gather Equipment:

- 6-quart (5.68 L) electric pressure cooker
- Measuring cups and spoons
- Cutting board
- Knife
- Wooden spoon
- Spice ball, cheesecloth, tea bag, or anything to make a spice pouch
- Slotted ladle
- Fine-mesh strainer
- 1 large stainless steel bowl
- 1 medium stainless steel bowl
- Medium pot

Prepare and Mise en Place Ingredients:

- 5 whole star anise
- 1½ sticks cinnamon
- 1½ tablespoons (22.5 mL) green cardamom pods
- 1 tablespoon (15 mL) coriander seeds
- 1½ teaspoons (7.5 mL) black peppercorns
- 1½ teaspoons (7.5 mL) vegetable oil
- ¼ cup (60 mL) Ginger-Garlic Masala (page 44)
- 1 medium yellow onion, peeled and cut in half
- 6 cups (1.5 L) water
- 900 g (2 lb) bone-in, skin-on chicken thighs
- 2 tablespoons (30 mL) brown sugar
- 2 tablespoons (30 mL) fish sauce
- 1½ tablespoons (22.5 mL) sriracha chili sauce, plus more to taste (optional)
- 225 g (8 oz) rice noodles
- 225 g (8 oz) bean sprouts
- ½ cup (125 mL) chopped fresh cilantro (optional)
- 1 whole jalapeno pepper, thinly sliced
- 6 sprigs fresh Thai basil (omit if you can't source)
- ½ cup (125 mL) chopped green onions
- Black pepper to taste
- 1 medium lime, cut in wedges

Substitution: Making this recipe vegetarian while keeping true to Vietnamese food culture is tricky. Vietnamese cooking doesn't make use of soy, or dairy, with the exception of Vietnamese people of Chinese descent. If you were to replace the chicken with a 796 mL (28 oz) can of drained kidney beans, black beans, or mung beans, you'd be keeping true to the cuisine. You may also replace the jalapeno with your favourite chili for Asian food if you want something with a bit more heat.

INSTRUCTIONS

1. Turn the electric pressure cooker on to Sauté. Once it's warm, add the star anise, cinnamon sticks, cardamom pods, coriander seeds, and peppercorns. Cook for 1–2 minutes, just enough to begin releasing the spices' natural oils. Press Cancel.

2. Remove the spices from the inner pot and place everything but the cinnamon sticks in a spice ball, cheesecloth, tea bag, or anything else you can use to make a spice pouch. Set the pouch and the cinnamon sticks aside.

3. Turn the electric pressure cooker on to Sauté. When it's hot, add the oil, Ginger-Garlic Masala, and onions. Sauté for 2–3 minutes.

4. Press Cancel. Add the water, spice pouch and cinnamon sticks from step 2, chicken, brown sugar, fish sauce, and sriracha (if using).

5. Place and seal the lid. Cook on the Soup/Broth setting for 1 hour.

6. Natural-release pressure for 10 minutes, then quick-release any remaining pressure.

7. Remove the lid. Using a slotted ladle, remove the chicken and place it in a bowl.

8. Using a fine-mesh strainer, strain the broth into a large mixing bowl to remove the onions, cinnamon sticks, and small particles. Discard the contents of the strainer.

9. Remove the skin and bones from the chicken and discard. Put the chicken back into the broth. Return the broth to the inner pot so you can reheat it using the Sauté setting, if needed.

10. On the stove, bring water to a boil in a medium pot.

11. Put the rice noodles in a fine-mesh strainer. Dip the noodles in the boiling water for 1 minute just to loosen them. Detangle and divide them among four bowls.

12. To the bowls with the noodles, add portion-sized amounts of the bean sprouts, cilantro (if fresh uncooked cilantro leaves don't leave a soapy taste in your mouth), jalapeno, Thai basil, and green onions, plus pepper to taste.

13. Add hot broth and chicken on top. Squeeze the juice from a lime wedge overtop and place the wedge in the broth. Add sriracha to taste. Let the noodles finish cooking in the hot broth.

Nutrition Facts
Vietnamese Chicken Pho
Per 2 cups (500 mL)

Calories 494

Calories from fat 108	
% Daily Value*	
Fat 12 g	18%
Saturated 3 g	19%
Polyunsaturated 3 g	
Monounsaturated 5 g	
Cholesterol 65 mg	22%
Sodium 1,217 mg	53%
Potassium 624 mg	18%
Carbohydrate 74 g	25%
Fibre 10 g	42%
Sugars 9 g	10%
Protein 27 g	54%
Vitamin A 750 iu	15%
Vitamin C 38 mg	46%
Calcium 170 mg	17%
Iron 7 mg	39%

*Percent Daily Values are based on a 2,000-calorie diet.

Electric Pressure Cooker Daal Stew

This is one of my favourite stews from my teen years when I was adopted by a Sikh household. My recipe is a bit on the medium-high side spice-wise. If you think it will be too spicy for you, make my Ginger-Garlic Masala without the serrano peppers and cut back on the amount of cayenne pepper you add.

PREP:	COOK:	NATURAL RELEASE:	TOTAL:	
20 minutes	10 minutes	15 minutes	45 minutes	

CUISINE:	HEAT INDEX:	STORAGE:	SERVINGS:	CALORIES PER SERVING:
Indian	Medium to high	Freeze, or jar at 11 lb (76 kPa) of pressure for 75 minutes	6 × 2 cups (500 mL)	327 kcal

Gather Equipment:

- 6-quart (5.68 L) electric pressure cooker
- Cutting board
- Knife or food processor with dicing blade
- Measuring cups and spoons
- Sieve
- Wooden spoon

Prepare and Mise en Place Ingredients:

- 2 tablespoons (30 mL) coconut oil (or ghee or extra-virgin olive oil)
- 1 medium yellow onion, diced
- 1 large russet potato, diced
- 1 cup (250 mL) diced celery
- 1 cup (250 mL) frozen cut green beans
- ½ cup (125 mL) diced carrots
- 1 tablespoon (15 mL) Ginger-Garlic Masala (page 44)
- 1 tablespoon (15 mL) Thana Jeeroo (page 46)
- 1½ teaspoons (7.5 mL) salt
- 1 teaspoon (5 mL) Garam Masala (page 47)
- 1 teaspoon (5 mL) ground cayenne pepper
- 1 teaspoon (5 mL) ground turmeric
- 4 cups (1 L) water
- 2 cups (500 mL) dried red lentils, rinsed
- 2 cups (500 mL) water

INSTRUCTIONS

1. Turn the electric pressure cooker on to Sauté. When it's hot, add the oil and onions. Sauté until the tips are lightly brown, about 2 minutes.

2. Add the potato, celery, green beans, and carrots. Sauté until the green beans start to defrost, about 2 minutes.

3. Add the Ginger-Garlic Masala, Thana Jeeroo, salt, Garam Masala, cayenne pepper, and turmeric. Sauté for 2 minutes.

4. Press Cancel. Add 4 cups (1 L) of water and deglaze the pot. Add the lentils.

5. Place and seal the lid. Cook at High Pressure for 2 minutes.

6. Natural-release for 5 minutes, then quick-release any remaining pressure.

7. Remove the lid. Add 2 cups (500 mL) of water. Stir well so that the lentils don't stick to the bottom.

8. Place and seal the lid. Cook at High Pressure for another 2 minutes.

9. Natural-release pressure for 10 minutes, then quick-release any remaining pressure. **Note:** You may need to add more water after it's done if it's really thick.

Nutrition Facts

Daal Stew
Per 2 cups (500 mL)

Calories 327

Calories from fat 54

% Daily Value*

Fat 6 g	9%
Saturated 4 g	25%
Trans 0 g	
Polyunsaturated 1 g	
Monounsaturated 1 g	
Cholesterol 0 mg	0%
Sodium 624 mg	27%
Potassium 1,010 mg	29%
Carbohydrate 53 g	18%
Fibre 21 g	88%
Sugars 4 g	4%
Protein 18 g	36%
Vitamin A 2,158 iu	43%
Vitamin C 12 mg	15%
Calcium 77 mg	8%
Iron 6 mg	33%

* Percent Daily Values are based on a 2,000-calorie diet.

Electric Pressure Cooker
Thai Chicken Panang Curry

Despite what you may be familiar with, Thai food that is traditionally served with rice, like this Thai curry, is not to be served with chopsticks. In Thai culture, dishes served with rice are eaten with a spoon, and a fork is used to guide the food on the spoon. The proper use of chopsticks in Asia is as varied as the many cultures and cuisines found within the continent. Panang curry is red curry but has more tones of sweetness than Thai Red Curry (page 137). It's also one of the many Thai curries that are traditionally served with rice.

Developing this recipe for the electric pressure cooker was challenging. Because the flavour profiles of Thai food involve a lot of cooking on direct heat, maintaining those flavours under pressure isn't easy. I tried my best to create a recipe that doesn't break my rule of storing chicken in 454-gram (1 lb) portions, but in the end it wasn't possible.

PREP:	COOK:	NATURAL RELEASE:	TOTAL:	
20 minutes	22 minutes	10 minutes	42 minutes	
CUISINE:	**HEAT INDEX:**	**STORAGE:**	**SERVINGS:**	**CALORIES PER**
Thai	Mild to medium	Freeze, or jar the curry at 11 lb (76 kPa) of pressure for 75 minutes and freeze the rice	6 × 1 cup (250 mL) with 1 cup (250 mL) rice	**SERVING:** 1,001 kcal

Gather Equipment:

- Two 6-quart (5.68 L) electric pressure cookers, or one 6-quart (5.68 L) electric pressure cooker and a second inner pot
- Measuring cups and spoons
- Cutting board
- Knife
- Garlic press
- Food processor or food chopper attachment for your immersion blender
- Can opener
- Wooden spoon

Prepare and Mise en Place Ingredients:

For the rice:

- 2½ cups (625 mL) jasmine rice, rinsed
- ½ cup (125 mL) black rice, rinsed
- 2 cups (500 mL) water
- 400 mL (14 oz) can full-fat coconut milk, stirred

For the curry:

- 1 tablespoon (15 mL) coconut oil
- ½ medium yellow onion, chopped
- 5 cloves garlic, minced or pressed
- 6 tablespoons (90 mL) panang curry paste
- 1 tablespoon (15 mL) unsalted sugar-free peanut butter
- 12 kaffir lime leaves, soaked, then bruised to release flavours
- 400 ml (14 oz) can full-fat coconut milk, stirred
- 3 tablespoons (45 mL) fish sauce
- 680 g (1.5 lb) boneless skinless chicken thighs, cubed
- 1 large red bell pepper, cut in thick slices
- 1 large orange bell pepper, cut in thick slices
- ¼ cup (60 mL) fresh Thai basil leaves (omit if you can't source)
- ¼ cup (60 mL) unsalted dry roasted peanuts, chopped

Note: If using two inner pots, the cook time and the natural release time will each increase by 10 minutes.

Substitution: To make this dish vegetarian, substitute 1½ cups (375 mL) cashews for the chicken. The time under pressure remains the same.

Tip: The black rice, panang curry paste, and kaffir lime leaves are available online if you live in a food desert.

INSTRUCTIONS

For the rice:

1. In a 6-quart (5.L) electric pressure cooker, in the following order, add the jasmine rice, black rice, water, and coconut milk. If using two inner pots with the same cooker, use the first inner pot.
2. Place and seal the lid. Set to High Pressure for 22 minutes.
3. Natural-release pressure for 10 minutes, then quick-release any remaining pressure.
4. Remove the lid and stir the rice. If using two inner pots, remove the inner pot holding the rice, cover, and set aside.

For the curry:

1. While the rice is cooking, turn the second 6-quart (5.68 L) electric pressure cooker on to Sauté. (If using a second inner pot, place it in the electric pressure cooker and turn on to Sauté.) Once it's hot, add the coconut oil, onions, and garlic. Sauté for about 1 minute.
2. Add the curry paste and peanut butter. Sauté for a couple of minutes. Press Cancel.
3. Add the kaffir lime leaves, coconut milk, and fish sauce. Give it a stir to thoroughly combine.
4. Add the chicken. Lightly break up the chicken so it's not a giant lump, but don't overmix it.
5. Place and seal the lid. Cook at High Pressure for 5 minutes.
6. Natural-release pressure for 10 minutes, then quick-release any remaining pressure.
7. Open the lid. Turn on to Sauté. Once it's simmering, add the sliced bell peppers. Cook for a couple of minutes if canning or 5 minutes if freezing. Press Cancel.
8. Add the Thai basil (if using) and peanuts. Stir.
9. Serve 1 cup (250 mL) curry with 1 cup (250 mL) rice.

Nutrition Facts

Thai Chicken Panang Curry
Per 1 cup (250 mL) + 1 cup (250 mL) rice

Calories 1,001

Calories from fat 378

% Daily Value*

Fat 42 g	65%
Saturated 30 g	188%
Polyunsaturated 2 g	
Monounsaturated 4 g	
Cholesterol 96 mg	32%
Sodium 1,762 mg	77%
Potassium 438 mg	13%
Carbohydrate 119 g	40%
Fibre 10 g	42%
Sugars 18 g	20%
Protein 41 g	82%
Vitamin A 2,250 iu	45%
Vitamin C 138.6 mg	168%
Calcium 70 mg	7%
Iron 4.1 mg	23%

*Percent Daily Values are based on a 2,000-calorie diet.

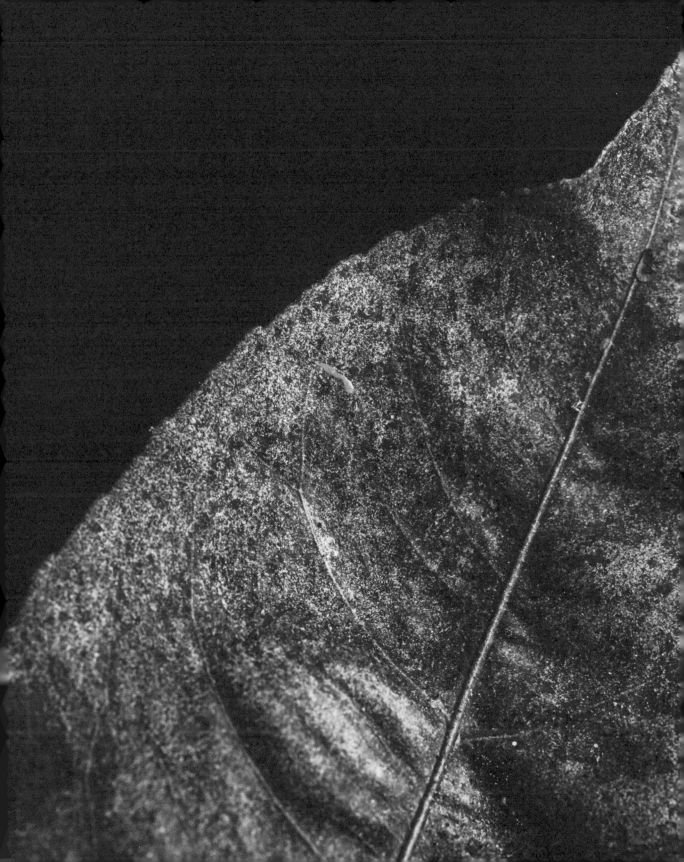

Electric Pressure Cooker
Thai Chicken Massaman Curry

Thai massaman curry has a long and rich history. It's also one of the rare examples of a fusion dish enjoyed by Western cultures that isn't the result of Western colonization. When Persia began trading with Thailand in the seventeenth century, it introduced a whole new set of spices and vegetables, including potatoes, to the local cuisine. Some of the spices introduced by Persia came by way of other Asian cuisines, such as the spices from the Indian subcontinent. The paste is a fusion of spices native to Persia, India, and Thailand.

This dish's name comes from the archaic Persian-derivative word for "Muslim": *mosalman*. This dish rose to such popularity that a prince of Siam (the former name of Thailand) wrote a poem in which the dish is personified as a lover.

I loved developing this recipe for the electric pressure cooker. Hopefully it continues to thrive for another four centuries with more people being able to access it.

PREP:	COOK:	NATURAL RELEASE:	TOTAL:	
20 minutes	22 minutes	10 minutes	42 minutes	
CUISINE:	**HEAT INDEX:**	**STORAGE:**	**SERVINGS:**	**CALORIES PER SERVING:**
Thai	Mild	Freeze, or jar the curry at 11 lb (76 kPa) of pressure for 75 minutes and freeze the rice	6 × 2 cups (500 mL) with 1 cup (250 mL) rice	1,103 kcal

Gather Equipment:

- Two 6-quart (5.68 L) electric pressure cookers, or one 6-quart (5.68 L) electric pressure cooker and a second inner pot
- Measuring cups and spoons
- Cutting board
- Knife
- Food processor or food chopper attachment for your immersion blender
- Can opener
- Wooden spoon

Prepare and Mise en Place Ingredients:

For the rice:
- 2½ cups (625 mL) jasmine rice, rinsed
- ½ cup (125 mL) black rice, rinsed
- 2 cups (500 mL) water
- 400 mL (14 oz) can full-fat coconut milk, stirred

For the curry:
- 3 tablespoons (45 mL) coconut oil
- 2 tablespoons (30 mL) Ginger-Garlic Masala (page 44)
- 1 medium yellow onion, chopped
- 6 tablespoons (90 mL) massaman curry paste
- 900 g (2 lb) boneless skinless chicken thighs, cubed
- Two 400 mL (14 oz) cans full-fat coconut milk, stirred
- 2 cups (500 mL) cubed russet potatoes
- 2 cups (500 mL) frozen cut green beans
- ¼ cup (60 mL) lime juice
- ¼ cup (60 mL) fish sauce
- ¼ cup (60 mL) brown sugar
- 1 red bell pepper, chopped
- ½ cup unsalted roasted peanuts

Note: If using two inner pots, the cook time and the natural release time will each increase by 10 minutes.

Substitution: To make this dish vegetarian, substitute 1½ cups (375 mL) cashews for the chicken. The time under pressure remains the same.

Tip: The black rice and massaman curry paste are available online if you live in a food desert.

INSTRUCTIONS
For the rice:
1. In a 6-quart (5.L) electric pressure cooker, in the following order, add the jasmine rice, the black rice, water, and coconut milk. If using two inner pots with the same cooker, use the first inner pot.
2. Place and seal the lid. Set to High Pressure for 22 minutes.
3. Natural-release pressure for 10 minutes, then quick-release any remaining pressure.
4. Remove the lid and stir the rice. If using two inner pots, remove the inner pot holding the rice, cover, and set aside.

For the curry:
1. While the rice is cooking, turn the second 6-quart (5.68 L) electric pressure cooker on to Sauté. (If using a second inner pot, place it in the electric pressure cooker and turn on to Sauté.) When it's hot, add the coconut oil, Ginger-Garlic Masala, and onions. Sauté until the onions are translucent, about 1–2 minutes.
2. Add the massaman curry paste. Sauté for about 1 minute. Press Cancel.
3. Add the chicken and stir until coated.
4. Add the coconut milk, stirring well so that there is liquid between the bottom of the electric pressure cooker and the chicken.
5. Add the potatoes, green beans, lime juice, fish sauce, and brown sugar.
6. Place and seal the lid. Set to High Pressure for 5 minutes.
7. Natural-release pressure for 10 minutes, then quick-release any remaining pressure.
8. Remove the lid. Add the bell pepper and peanuts. Stir. Cover for about 5 minutes to allow the peppers to cook slightly.
9. Serve 2 cups (500 mL) curry with 1 cup (250 mL) rice.

Nutrition Facts
Thai Chicken Massaman Curry
Per 2 cups (500 mL) + 1 cup (250 mL) rice

Calories 1,103
Calories from fat 477
% Daily Value*

Fat 53 g	82%
Saturated 38 g	238%
Trans 1 g	
Polyunsaturated 4 g	
Monounsaturated 7 g	
Cholesterol 144 mg	48%
Sodium 988 mg	43%
Potassium 1,378 g	39%
Carbohydrate 115 g	38%
Fibre 9 g	38%
Sugars 19 g	21%
Protein 46 g	92%
Vitamin A 918 iu	18%
Vitamin C 43 mg	52%
Calcium 116 mg	12%
Iron 6 mg	33%

*Percent Daily Values are based on a 2,000-calorie diet.

The Best Roast Chicken
You Will Ever Have, 3 Ways:
Oven, Pressure Cooker, or Air Fryer

Roast chicken is comfort for many people with a western European background. It's a meal synonymous with Sunday family gatherings. It's also one of the first meals to be lost if someone's disability makes cooking with an oven unsafe.

I have developed this recipe to be cooked three different ways. If crisp skin is important to you, then cook it either in the oven or in an air fryer that has a rotisserie. The oven recipe calls for basting, but that is completely optional. The basting instructions are there only to create added flavour for the gravy drippings. Using the rotisserie in an oven-style air fryer does this job. And if you are one to toss the skin, then use the electric pressure cooker method for the easiest and quickest cooking with all the flavour.

PREP:	OVEN:	ELECTRIC PRESSURE COOKER:	OVEN-STYLE AIR FRYER:	TOTAL:
20 minutes	1 hour, 20 minutes	24 minutes + 10 minutes natural release	50 minutes–1 hour, 10 minutes	54 minutes–1 hour, 40 minutes
CUISINE:	**HEAT INDEX:**	**STORAGE:**	**SERVINGS:**	**CALORIES PER SERVING:**
Western European	None	Eat within 3 days or freeze	4	469 kcal with gravy

Gather Equipment:
- Measuring cups and spoons
- Cutting board
- Knife
- Bamboo skewers or food-safe twine
- Regular spoon
- Meat thermometer or probe
- Platter
- Aluminum foil
- Sauce pot

For oven method:
- Roasting pan

For electric pressure cooker method:
- 6-quart (5.68 L) electric pressure cooker
- Trivet

For oven-style air fryer rotisserie method:
- Air fryer oven
- Rotisserie rod
- Drip pan

Prepare and Mise en Place Ingredients:
- 1.8 kg (4 lb) fryer/roasting chicken (approx)
- 2 cups (500 mL) salt-free chicken broth, divided in 2 if cooking in the air fryer
- 2 teaspoons (10 mL) black pepper (or more to taste), divided in 2 for oven and pressure cooker methods
- 2 teaspoons (10 mL) salt (or more to taste), divided in 2 for oven and pressure cooker methods
- 1 medium lemon, cut in quarters
- 4 cloves garlic, smashed with the flat blade of a knife and sliced
- 6 sprigs fresh parsley
- 3 sprigs fresh rosemary
- 3 sprigs fresh thyme
- 3 sprigs fresh sage
- ½ cup (125 mL) Herb Butter (page 50)
- 2 tablespoons (30 mL) cornstarch mixed with 2 tablespoons (30 mL) cold water

OVEN – INSTRUCTIONS

1. Preheat the oven to 375°F (190°C).

2. In the roasting pan, add the chicken broth, 1 teaspoon (5 mL) of the black pepper and 1 teaspoon (5 mL) of the salt.

3. Stuff the chicken with the lemon, garlic, parsley, rosemary, thyme, and sage.

4. Secure the opening of the cavity with the bamboo skewer or twine.

5. Loosen the skin of the chicken from its body. Using a regular spoon, put the Herb Butter between the chicken meat and the skin. From the outside of the skin, smoosh the butter around under the skin so that it covers most of the top of the chicken. You can also add some to the top of the legs and the loosened skin between the legs and the body of the chicken. Insert the meat thermometer or probe. The probe should be inserted about 2.5 cm (1 inch) into the thickest part of the breast, making sure to not touch any bones.

6. Place the chicken in the oven and cook to an internal temperature of 165°F (74°C), approximately 1 hour and 20 minutes, depending on the size of the chicken. Every 20 minutes, remove it from the oven and baste, making sure to cover the top of the chicken with the drippings. If you don't have the physical ability to baste the chicken, sprinkle the top of the chicken with salt and pepper and add some Herb Butter to the roasting pan before placing it in the oven.

7. Once it's done cooking, remove the chicken from the oven and place it on a deep serving platter. It's important that the platter is such that it will be easy to pour the extra juices the chicken will release into a sauce pot.

8. Cover the chicken with aluminum foil. It should sit for about 20 minutes. It's during this time that I throw my side dishes—potatoes for mashed potatoes and whatever veg—into the electric pressure cooker to steam.

9. While the chicken is sitting, put the drippings into a sauce pot and add the remaining 1 teaspoon (5 mL) each of pepper and salt. On medium-high heat, bring it to a boil.

10. Reduce to medium heat. Add the cornstarch-and-water mixture to make gravy. It will immediately begin to thicken. Whisk well until most of the fat is incorporated.

11. Reduce to low heat. After the chicken has been sitting for about 10 minutes, remove the aluminum foil and pour the drippings from the bottom of the serving platter into the sauce pot with the gravy. Mix again. Re-cover the chicken with the foil.

12. After a total of about 20 minutes' sitting time, remove the aluminum foil and carve the chicken. During this process, and when the legs fall off, it will re-lease more drippings. Add those drippings to the gravy and mix well.

13. Freeze the carcass with the lemon, herbs, and garlic together to use for Chicken Soup (page 153).

ELECTRIC PRESSURE COOKER – INSTRUCTIONS

1. In the pressure cooker's inner pot, place the trivet. Add the chicken broth, 1 teaspoon (5 mL) of the black pepper and 1 teaspoon (5 mL) of the salt.

2. Stuff the chicken with the lemon, garlic, parsley, rosemary, thyme, and sage.

3. Secure the opening of the cavity with the bamboo skewer or twine.

4. Loosen the skin of the chicken from its body. Using a regular spoon, put the Herb Butter between the chicken meat and the skin. From the outside of the skin, smoosh the butter around under the skin so that it covers most of the top of the chicken. You can also add some to the top of the legs and the loosened skin between the legs and the body of the chicken.

5. Place the chicken on the trivet.

6. Place and seal the lid. Cook at High Pressure for 24 minutes. If your chicken isn't 1.8 kg (4 lb), cook for 6 minutes per 454 g (1 lb).

7. Natural-release pressure for 10 minutes, then quick-release any remaining pressure.

8. Remove the chicken from the pressure cooker and place it on a platter. Cover the chicken with aluminum foil and let it sit for at least 20 minutes.

9. Turn the pressure cooker on to Sauté. Add the remaining 1 teaspoon (5 mL) each of pepper and salt. Once the contents are boiling, add the cornstarch-and-water mixture to make gravy. It will immediately begin to thicken. Whisk well until most of the fat is incorporated.

10. After about 20 minutes' sitting time, remove the aluminum foil and carve the chicken. During this process, and when the legs fall off, it will release more drippings. Add those drippings to the gravy and mix well.

11. Freeze the carcass with the lemon, herbs, and garlic together to use for Chicken Soup (page 153).

OVEN-STYLE AIR FRYER ROTISSERIE – INSTRUCTIONS

1. Stuff the chicken with the lemon, garlic, parsley, rosemary, thyme, and sage.

2. Secure the opening of the cavity with the bamboo skewer or twine.

3. Loosen the skin of the chicken from its body. Using a regular spoon, put the Herb Butter between the chicken meat and the skin. From the outside of the skin, smoosh the butter around under the skin so that it covers most of the top of the chicken. You can also add some to the top of the legs and the loosened skin between the legs and the body of the chicken.

4. Insert the rotisserie rod through the opening at the neck and out the back end. Secure it firmly in place using the prongs and screws that came with the rotisserie rods. If you are unsure about this process, refer to the illustrations in the manufacturer's user guide.

5. With the chicken on the rod, place the rod in the rotisserie slots in the oven. Place the air fryer's drip pan under the chicken. Add 1 cup (250 mL) of the chicken broth to the pan.

6. Using the Air Fry plus Rotate setting, set to 350°F (175°C) for 1 hour and 10 minutes. Cook to an internal temperature of 165°F (74°C), approximately 50 minutes to 1 hour and 10 minutes, depending on size. When 50 minutes has elapsed, check the temperature every 10 minutes. The probe/thermometer should be inserted about 2.5 cm (1 inch) into the thickest part of the breast, making sure to not touch any bones.

7. Remove the chicken from the air fryer and place it on a platter. Cover the chicken with aluminum foil and let it sit for at least 20 minutes.

8. While the chicken is sitting, put the drippings from the drip pan into a sauce pot and add the remaining 1 cup (250 mL) of chicken broth, 2 teaspoons (10 mL) salt, and 2 teaspoons (10 mL) pepper. On medium-high heat, bring it to a boil.

9. Reduce to medium heat. Add the cornstarch-and-water mixture to make gravy. It will immediately begin to thicken. Whisk well until most of the fat is incorporated.

10. Reduce to low heat. After the chicken has been sitting for about 10 minutes, remove the aluminum foil and pour the drippings from the bottom of the serving platter into the sauce pot with the gravy. Mix again. Re-cover the chicken with the foil.

11. After about a total of 20 minutes' sitting time, remove the aluminum foil and carve the chicken. During this process, and when the legs fall off, it will release more drippings. Add those drippings to the gravy and mix well.

12. Freeze the carcass with the lemon, herbs, and garlic together to use for Chicken Soup (page 153).

Nutrition Facts

The Best Roast Chicken You Will Ever Have
Per ¼ chicken (with gravy)

Calories 469

Calories from fat 315

% Daily Value*

Fat 35 g	54%
Saturated 14 g	88%
Polyunsaturated 1 g	
Monounsaturated 8 g	
Cholesterol 144 mg	48%
Sodium 1,584 mg	69%
Potassium 143 mg	4%
Carbohydrate 11 g	4%
Fibre 3 g	13%
Sugars 1 g	1%
Protein 31 g	62%
Vitamin A 1,100 iu	22%
Vitamin C 49.5 mg	60%
Calcium 60 mg	6%
Iron 2.7 mg	15%

*Percent Daily Values are based on a 2,000-calorie diet.

Air Fryer Potato Scones with Bonus Oven Method

My maternal grandmother was Scottish. Potato scones are a staple in Scottish homes and a great way to use up leftover mashed potatoes. Every time we had leftover mashed potatoes, fresh-out-of-the-oven potato scones with jam and maple syrup were the dessert. My wheelchair doesn't allow for baking in an oven, so I had to adapt this recipe for the air fryer. You can also make a savoury version by making bacon bits and adding it to the dough.

PREP:	OVEN-STYLE AIR FRYER:	COMBO-STYLE AIR FRYER:	TOTAL:	
20 minutes	14–16 minutes	16–18 minutes	34–38 minutes	
CUISINE:	**HEAT INDEX:**	**STORAGE:**	**SERVINGS:**	**CALORIES PER SERVING:**
Scottish	None	Eat within 3 days or freeze	4 (8 for oven version)	199 kcal

Gather Equipment:

- Oven-style air fryer or 8-quart (7.57 L) electric pressure cooker– air fryer combo
- Measuring cups and spoons
- Mixing bowls
- Pastry blender or a couple of butter knives
- Trivet and the bottom of a spring-form pan if using combo cooker

Prepare and Mise en Place Ingredients:

- 1 cup plus 3 tablespoons (280 mL) all-purpose flour (approx)
- ½ tablespoon (7.5 mL) baking powder
- ½ teaspoon (2.5 mL) salt
- 1½ tablespoons (22.5 mL) cold unsalted butter, cut in small cubes
- ½ cup (120 mL) mashed potatoes (made with unsalted butter and milk)
- 3 tablespoons (45 mL) milk
- 1 egg
- 1 tablespoon (15 mL) flour for kneading

Tip: The scones are best served warm with butter and jam or maple syrup.

INSTRUCTIONS

1. In a mixing bowl, blend the flour, baking powder, and salt.
2. Add the butter cubes to the flour mixture. Using the pastry blender, or a couple of butter knives like Wolverine blades, cut the butter into the flour mixture until you have tiny pea-sized chunks of butter and flour.
3. In another mixing bowl, blend the mashed potatoes, milk, and egg.
4. Add the wet ingredients to the dry ingredients. Mix well until you have a dry, crumbly dough.
5. Knead the dough. If the dough is sticky, add the second quantity of flour and knead until the dough is soft and no longer sticky.
6. Roll the dough into a log. Cut the log into 4 pieces. Turn those pieces into circles about 2.5 cm (1 inch) in height.

If using an oven-style air fryer:

1. Place the scones on the bottom rack in the air fryer oven.

2. Using the Bake function, set to 350°F (175°C) for 12 minutes. Flip the scones and air fry for another 2–4 minutes using the same settings.

3. Remove the scones from air fryer. Let them cool for a bit.

If using an electric pressure cooker–air fryer combo:

1. Add the trivet to the bottom of the pot. Place the bottom of a springform pan on top of the trivet. Place the scones on top of the pan.

2. Place the air fryer lid. Air fry on the Bake setting at 350°F (175°C) for 14 minutes. Flip the scones and air fry for another 2–4 minutes.

3. Remove the scones from the air fryer. Let them cool for a bit.

Bonus Oven Method

Gather Equipment:

- Oven
- Measuring cups and spoons
- Mixing bowls
- Pastry blender or a couple of butter knives
- Baking sheet

Prepare and Mise en Place Ingredients:

- 2 cups (474 mL) all-purpose flour (approx)
- 1 tablespoon (15 mL) baking powder
- 1 teaspoon (5 mL) salt
- 3 tablespoons (45 mL) cold unsalted butter, cut in small cubes
- 1 cup (236 mL) mashed potatoes (made with unsalted butter and milk)
- ⅓ cup (80 mL) milk
- 1 egg
- 1 tablespoon (15 mL) flour for kneading

INSTRUCTIONS

1. Preheat the oven to 400°F (200°C).
2. In a mixing bowl, blend the flour, baking powder, and salt.
3. Add the butter cubes to the flour mixture. Using the pastry blender, or a couple of butter knives like Wolverine blades, cut the butter into the flour mixture until you have tiny pea-sized chunks of butter and flour.
4. In another mixing bowl, blend the mashed potatoes, milk, and egg.
5. Add the wet ingredients to the dry ingredients. Mix well until you have a dry, crumbly dough.
6. Knead the dough. If the dough is sticky, add the second quantity of flour and knead until the dough is soft and no longer sticky.
7. Roll the dough into a log. Cut the log into 8 pieces. Turn those pieces into circles about 2.5 cm (1 inch) in height.
8. Place the scones on a baking sheet. Put the sheet on the middle rack in the oven.
9. Bake for 15–18 minutes or until golden brown.
10. Remove the scones from the oven. Let them cool for a bit. Best served warm.

Nutrition Facts

Potato Scones
Per 1 scone

Calories 199

Calories from fat 54		
% Daily Value*		
Fat 6 g		9%
Saturated 3 g		19%
Cholesterol 59 mg		20%
Sodium 511 mg		22%
Potassium 144 mg		4%
Carbohydrate 30 g		10%
Fibre 1 g		4%
Sugars 1 g		1%
Protein 6 g		12%
Vitamin A 217 iu		4%
Vitamin C 1 mg		1%
Calcium 113 mg		11%
Iron 2 mg		11%

*Percent Daily Values are based on a 2,000-calorie diet.

AIR FRYER SWEET POTATO AND BUTTERNUT SQUASH HASH WITH POACHED EGG

We all have dishes that, if we suddenly couldn't access them, would take part of our soul because they are so integral to our food cultures. While working on this book, I was having a challenging time developing recipes that were American, as in from the Unites States. I always find it fascinating that we share so much with our southern neighbours and yet our food cultures are very distinct. This is the result of our different histories around colonization. When it comes to American food, there is also the history of how enslaved Black people influenced the cuisine.

I asked some of my American friends from a variety of backgrounds to give me three dishes that would devastate them if disability meant they could no longer prepare them. Hash was one dish that came up that filled the American-recipe gap for this book. The closer to the American South one grows up, the more hash becomes one of those important foods. Hash also becomes an important dish in areas that once had a high population of indentured Irish servants. This isn't by accident.

Hash was one of those foods that kept enslaved people and indentured servants fuelled. It is cheap to make and high in energy. Once hash houses gained popularity throughout the United States, the dish became a staple among low-income households and something looked down on by those with money. And as with many of the other foods in this book, this history has been whitewashed and the classism erased.

Hash is a testament to colonization, enslavement, and the tenacity of oppressed people.

Air Fryer Sweet Potato and Butternut Squash Hash with Poached Egg

I developed this hash recipe based on cheap, in-season ingredients that are native to the Americas and traditionally used in southern US and Irish American cuisines. When butternut squash isn't in season, feel free to substitute whatever squash is in season, or a fleshy fruit such as pear.

PREP:	OVEN-STYLE AIR FRYER:	COMBO-STYLE AIR FRYER:	TOTAL:	
25 minutes	37–39 minutes	48–52 minutes	1 hour, 2 minutes–1 hour, 17 minutes	

CUISINE:	HEAT INDEX:	STORAGE:	SERVINGS:	CALORIES PER SERVING:
Southern and Irish American	Mild	Eat within 3 days or freeze	4 × 1½ cups (375 mL) with 1 egg	315 kcal

Gather Equipment:

- 8-quart (7.57 L) oven-style air fryer with rotisserie basket or electric pressure cooker–air fryer combo with basket and trivet
- Measuring spoons
- Vegetable peeler
- Cutting board
- Knife
- Mixing bowl
- Tongs
- Four ¾ cup (185 mL) ramekins
- Non-stick cooking spray
- Parchment paper if using a combo-style air fryer with a non-stick inner pot

Prepare and Mise en Place Ingredients:

- 2 tablespoons (30 mL) extra-virgin olive oil
- 1 teaspoon (5 mL) salt
- 1 teaspoon (5 mL) ground turmeric
- 1 teaspoon (5 mL) sweet paprika
- ½ teaspoon (2.5 mL) ground cayenne pepper (or black pepper)
- 1 butternut squash, peeled, seeded, and cut in small cubes
- 1 large sweet potato, peeled and cut in small cubes
- 1 red bell pepper, seeded and diced
- 1 small red onion, diced
- 4 large eggs
- 8 tablespoons water (120 mL), divided in 4

INSTRUCTIONS

For Oven-Style Air Fryer

1. In a mixing bowl, add the olive oil, salt, turmeric, paprika, and cayenne pepper. Stir well.
2. Add the squash, sweet potato, bell pepper, and onion. Using the tongs, toss well.
3. Put the mixture into the rotisserie basket and place the basket in the air fryer's rotisserie slots.
4. Using the Air Fry and Rotate settings, cook at 400°F (200°C) for 30 minutes.
5. When it's done, remove the basket and let the hash sit in the basket to continue cooking while you do the eggs.
6. Spray each ramekin with non-stick cooking spray.
7. Put 1 egg into each of the 4 ramekins. Add 2 tablespoons (30 mL) water to each ramekin.

8. Place the bottom rack into the air fryer oven. Using the Air Fry setting, set to 360°F (180°C) for 9 minutes. Wait for the oven to preheat.

9. When the Add Food indicator goes off, put the ramekins on the bottom rack of the air fryer.

10. Cook for 7–9 minutes, depending on how yolky you want the egg.

11. Remove the hash from the basket. Divide it among four plates and serve with 1 egg each.

For Electric Pressure Cooker – Air Fryer Combo

1. In a mixing bowl, add the olive oil, salt, turmeric, paprika, and cayenne pepper. Stir well.

2. Add the squash, sweet potato, bell pepper, and onion. Using the tongs, toss well.

3. Put the mixture into the air fryer basket and place the basket in the cooker's inner pot. If your inner pot isn't non-stick, add parchment paper to the bottom of the inner pot before inserting the fryer basket.

4. Using the Air Fry setting, cook at 400°F (200°C) for 38 minutes.

5. When it's done, remove the basket and let the hash sit in the basket to continue cooking while you do the eggs.

6. Spray each ramekin with non-stick cooking spray.

7. Put 1 egg into each of the 4 ramekins. Add 2 tablespoons (30 mL) water to each ramekin.

8. Place the trivet in the inner pot. Put the ramekins on the trivet.

9. Using the Air Fry setting, cook at 360°F (180°C) for 10–14 minutes, depending on how yolky you want the egg.

10. Remove the hash from the basket. Divide it among four plates and serve with 1 egg each.

Nutrition Facts

Sweet Potato and Butternut Squash Hash with Poached Egg
Per 1 ½ cups (375 mL) + 1 egg

Calories 315

Calories from fat 108	
% Daily Value*	
Fat 12 g	18%
Saturated 3 g	19%
Trans 1 g	
Polyunsaturated 2 g	
Monounsaturated 7 g	
Cholesterol 186 mg	62%
Sodium 710 mg	31%
Potassium 1,148 mg	33%
Carbohydrate 44 g	15%
Fibre 8 g	33%
Sugars 10 g	11%
Protein 10 g	20%
Vitamin A 22,543 iu	671%
Vitamin C 82 mg	99%
Calcium 155 mg	16%
Iron 3 mg	17%

*Percent Daily Values are based on a 2,000-calorie diet.

ALL YOUR "SPOONS"

Electric Pressure Cooker Chicken Dum Biryani

Chicken Dum Biryani is one of my favourites. It took a lot of experimenting to get this recipe exactly right for the electric pressure cooker and to be true to what makes something a *dum pukht*. For a dish to be a *dum* (on a slow fire or slowly with steam) *pukht* (cook), it needs to be slowly cooked with steam inside a well-sealed container. This dish is cooked under high pressure, so why the *dum*? Because unlike other recipes where you can quick-release any remaining pressure after 10 minutes, this recipe must be allowed a full natural release of pressure, creating the slow-cook-with-steam process but without the long times associated with traditional methods.

PREP:	MARINATE:	COOK:	NATURAL RELEASE:	TOTAL:
30 minutes	30 minutes	16 minutes	Full	1 hour 16 minutes + natural release

CUISINE:	HEAT INDEX:	STORAGE:	SERVINGS:	CALORIES PER SERVING:
Indian	Medium to high	Freeze	6 × 1 cup (250 mL)	281 kcal

Gather Equipment:

- 6-quart (5.68 L) electric pressure cooker
- Cutting board
- Knife
- Measuring cups and spoons
- Mixing bowls
- Wooden spoon

Prepare and Mise en Place Ingredients:

For the marinade:

- ½ cup (125 mL) full-fat Greek yogourt
- ¼ cup (60 mL) fresh mint, chopped
- 1 jalapeno pepper, diced
- 2 tablespoons (30 mL) Ginger-Garlic Masala (page 44)
- 2 teaspoons (10 mL) Garam Masala (page 47)
- 1 teaspoon (5 mL) salt
- 1 teaspoon (5 mL) ground coriander
- 1 teaspoon (5 mL) ground turmeric
- ¼ teaspoon (1.25 mL) ground cayenne pepper
- ¼ teaspoon (1.25 mL) green cardamom seeds
- ⅛ teaspoon (pinch) ground cloves
- 454 g (1 lb) boneless skinless chicken thighs, cut in bite-sized pieces

For the biryani:

- 2 tablespoons (30 mL) ghee (or unsalted butter)
- 5 black peppercorns
- 5 green cardamom pods
- 4 whole cloves
- 1 stick cinnamon
- 1 small yellow onion, thinly sliced
- 4 cloves garlic, crushed
- 1 jalapeno pepper, diced
- 1 tablespoon (15 mL) minced ginger
- 1 cup (250 mL) basmati rice, rinsed
- 1 cup (250 mL) water
- ¼ teaspoon (1.25 mL) salt

Substitution: To make this vegetarian, substitute 1 cup (250 mL) cubed Paneer (page 59) for the chicken. Marinate it as you would the chicken. Change the time under pressure to 4 minutes.

Tip: This recipe is on the medium-hot side of the spiciness scale. To reduce the heat, do any or all of the following: serve it with Greek yogourt; serve it with roti, naan, or another flatbread; seed the jalapeno peppers and/or reduce the amount—for example, use only ½ pepper in the marinade and ½ pepper in the biryani.

INSTRUCTIONS

For the marinade:

1. In a mixing bowl, add the following: yogourt, mint, jalapeno, Ginger-Garlic Masala, Garam Masala, salt, coriander, turmeric, cayenne pepper, cardamom seeds, and ground cloves. Mix well.
2. Add the chicken. Mix until the chicken is well coated.
3. Cover the bowl and put it in the fridge for a minimum of 30 minutes. It can even be put in the fridge overnight.

For the biryani:

1. Turn the electric pressure cooker on to Sauté. Once it's hot, add the ghee. Once the ghee starts to shimmer, add the peppercorns, cardamom pods, whole cloves, and cinnamon stick. Sauté for 1–2 minutes or until you hear the spices start to sizzle.
2. Add the onions and sauté for another 2–5 minutes, until the edges of the onions start to become brown or crispy. Do not completely caramelize the onions.
3. Add the garlic, jalapeno, and ginger and sauté for an additional 1–3 minutes, until the onions are completely caramelized. Press Cancel on the electric pressure cooker to turn it off.
4. Dump the marinated chicken into the pressure cooker and spread it out in a nice even layer.
5. Add the rice on top of the chicken, distributing it evenly.
6. Add the water. The rice should be completely submerged. If the rice is not submerged, spread it out. Be careful not to push the rice to the bottom of the pot, or you will get a burn warning. Sprinkle ¼ teaspoon (1.25 mL) salt evenly on top of the rice.
7. Place and seal the lid. Cook at High Pressure for 6 minutes.
8. Let all the pressure naturally release. Do not use the quick release.
9. When all the pressure has released, remove the lid and serve.

Nutrition Facts
Chicken Dum Biryani
Per 1 cup (250 mL)

Calories 281

Calories from fat 81

% Daily Value*

Fat 9 g	14%
Saturated 4 g	25%
Trans 1 g	
Polyunsaturated 1 g	
Monounsaturated 1 g	
Cholesterol 86 mg	29%
Sodium 468 mg	20%
Potassium 320 mg	9%
Carbohydrate 31 g	10%
Fibre 2 g	8%
Sugars 1 g	1%
Protein 19 g	38%
Vitamin A 179 iu	4%
Vitamin C 9 mg	11%
Calcium 59 mg	6%
Iron 2 mg	11%

*Percent Daily Values are based on a 2,000-calorie diet.

ELECTRIC PRESSURE COOKER DOUKHOBOR BORSHCH

My second dad was Doukhobor. Doukhobors are a Russian religious and ethnic group who fled persecution in Russia for their spiritual beliefs and found a home in Canada. At first they were welcomed by the Canadian government to farm as they pleased in the prairies of Saskatchewan. Soon, the Canadian government changed its mind about the Doukhobor people, and they had to relocate to British Columbia.

Again, things would repeat. At first they were welcomed. Then, Doukhobor children were forcibly removed from their families to be educated in the "proper" Western ways of the world. People were placed in concentration camps, including members of my family. It was a forced assimilation. It wasn't the first branch of my family tree to be treated in such a way.

This resulted in acts of protest and violence. After hundreds of years of (waves hands all over the place) *this*, many in the community had had enough. They were simply a group of farmers who believed in communal living and wanted to be left alone to live in concert with the land.

Doukhobor borshch is a staple dish of a group of people who have spent hundreds of years persisting. It sustains families during long, harsh winters. And it takes *hours* of painstaking labour to make. Hours of peeling potatoes and cooking them in more than one way. Hours of boiling jarred tomatoes from the summer harvest into a thick sauce. Hours of chopping carrots in multiple ways. Hours of chopping cabbage, bell peppers, celery, green onions, fresh dill, and more. Thankfully, it no longer takes hours to churn all the butter and collect thick cream, make the sour cream, and wait for cheese to cure. It takes hours to cook it once all the veg is prepared. It takes a team of people to cook it. Thankfully, it requires only one beet that is boiled to death and removed before serving.

Growing up with a Doukhobor dad meant spending my summers in Nelson, British Columbia, at my baba and deda's house (grandma and grandpa).

They were farmers. I wish I could say that goes without saying. They farmed honey. I could tell you stories about my deda gathering honeycombs first thing in the morning, bringing them down into the basement into barrels that had these spinner things, and extracting fresh honey that we'd have with our breakfast. You haven't lived until you've eaten fresh honeycomb.

My summers were spent climbing trees, roaming railway tracks in knicker-bockers, and having cousins trick me into thinking they were playing music videos on the TV by pretending to insert eight-tracks into the back of it. They were spent watching my baba spend hours jarring fresh fruits and veg from the farm, baking bread, and making borshch. So much borshch. Her kitchen was a warm hug, and if we were lucky, we were allowed to help her.

It was a nice reprieve from everything else. I don't remember anyone being there but my cousins and baba and deda, and the food.

In my adulthood, I always wanted to make borshch. To make someone borshch means you love them. Much of the economy in the Nelson and Grand Forks area of British Columbia is based on borshch, an integral part of a people's culture that the government tried to assimilate out of them.

The problem with borshch is it takes five hours to make, at least. When I finally learned the magic of cooking with an electric pressure cooker and could once again cook after becoming disabled, I made it one of my life's missions to convert Doukhobor borshch into something more manageable while still preserving the flavours.

The different ways one must cook the cabbage, the different ways of preparing the tomatoes, the different ways of preparing the potatoes, when one must add the mashed potatoes, and the different times the cream and butter get added all result in the final flavour. Change it slightly and the dish's complex flavours fall apart.

I wanted to crack this nut not only so that I could once again wrap myself in this warm blanket that played a foundational role in who I am, not only to make it accessible to people with disabilities, especially Doukhobor people, but also to help preserve such an important cultural dish.

Electric Pressure Cooker Doukhobor Borshch

This classic dish is worth every "spoon" it takes to make it. As a bonus, serve it with cubes of aged cheddar cheese or sour cream and a sprig of fresh dill.

PREP: 45 minutes	**COOK:** 30 minutes	**NATURAL RELEASE:** 10 minutes	**TOTAL:** 1 hour, 25 minutes
CUISINE: Doukhobor	**HEAT INDEX:** None	**STORAGE:** Freeze, or jar at 11 lb (76 kPa) of pressure for 60 minutes	**SERVINGS:** 12 × 1 cup (250 mL)	**CALORIES PER SERVING:** 299 kcal

Gather Equipment:

- 3-quart (2.84 L) electric pressure cooker or saucepan
- 6-quart (5.68 L) electric pressure cooker
- Cutting board
- Knife
- Carrot peeler
- Food processor
- Food grater with fine holes
- Measuring cups and spoons
- Can opener
- Stainless steel mixing bowls
- Potato masher
- Tongs
- Slotted ladle

Prepare and Mise en Place Ingredients:

- ½ cup plus 2 tablespoons (150 mL) unsalted butter, divided into ¼ cup (60 mL), 1 tablespoon (15 mL), ¼ cup (60 mL), and 1 tablespoon (15 mL)
- 1 cup (250 mL) chopped yellow onions, divided into ¾ cup (185 mL) and ¼ cup (60 mL)
- ¾ cup (180 mL) chopped green peppers, divided into 3 × ¼ cup (60 mL)
- ½ cup (125 mL) finely grated carrots
- 796 mL (28 oz) can crushed tomatoes
- 5 cups (1.25 L) shredded cabbage, divided into 2 cups (500 mL) and 3 cups (750 mL)
- 6 cups (1.5 L) water
- 1 tablespoon (15 mL) salt
- 4 medium russet potatoes, peeled and cut in half
- 1 small beet, peeled
- ½ cup (125 mL) chopped carrots
- ¼ cup (60 mL) chopped celery
- 1 cup (236 mL) whipping cream, divided in 2
- ¾ cup (185 mL) chopped green onions, divided into ¼ cup (60 mL) and ½ cup (125 mL)
- 2 tablespoons (30 mL) fresh chopped dill (or 1 tablespoon dried dill), divided in 2
- 1 cup (250 mL) diced potatoes
- Black pepper (to taste)

INSTRUCTIONS

1. Turn the 3-quart (2.84 L) electric pressure cooker on to Sauté. If using a saucepan, heat to medium.

2. Once it's hot, add ¼ cup (60 mL) of the butter, ¾ cup (185 mL) of the chopped onions, ¼ cup (60 mL) of the chopped green peppers, and the finely grated carrots. Sauté until the onions are transparent. Do not brown.

3. In the same electric pressure cooker or saucepan, add the crushed tomatoes, 1 tablespoon of the butter, and the remaining ¼ cup (60 mL) of chopped onions. Simmer until thick, about 5 minutes. Press Cancel.

4. Pour the contents into a storage container and set aside. Put the inner pot back into the pressure cooker.

5. Turn the 3-quart (2.84 L) pressure cooker on to Sauté, or the saucepan to medium. When it's hot, add 2 cups (500 mL) of the shredded cabbage with ¼ cup (60 mL) of the butter. Sauté until tender. Do not brown. Press Cancel when done.

6. In the 6-quart (5.68 L) electric pressure cooker, add the water, salt, halved potatoes, beet, chopped carrots, chopped celery, and ½ the sauce from step 4.

7. Place and seal the lid. Set to High Pressure for 10 minutes.

8. Quick-release the pressure.

9. Remove the lid. Remove the potatoes and mash with the remaining 1 tablespoon (15 mL) of butter, ½ cup (120 mL) of the whipping cream, ¼ cup (60 mL) of the chopped green peppers, ¼ cup (60 mL) of the chopped green onions, and 1 tablespoon (15 mL) of the fresh dill (or ½ tablespoon/7.5 mL dried dill). Set aside.

10. In the 6-quart (5.68 L) electric pressure cooker, add the diced potatoes and the remaining 3 cups (750 mL) of shredded cabbage.

11. Place and seal the lid. Set to High Pressure for 5 minutes.

12. Quick-release the pressure.

13. Remove the lid. Add the mashed potatoes from step 9 into the electric pressure cooker.

14. Place and seal the lid. Set to High Pressure for 5 minutes.

15. Natural-release pressure for 10 minutes, then quick-release any remaining pressure.

16. Remove the lid. Add the remaining ½ cup (120 mL) of whipping cream, the remainder of the sauce from step 4, the sautéed cabbage from step 5, the remaining ½ cup (125 mL) of chopped green onions, the remaining ¼ cup (60 mL) of chopped green peppers, and the remaining 1 tablespoon (15 mL) of fresh dill (or ½ tablespoon/7.5 mL dried dill).

17. Discard the whole beet. Season to taste with black pepper.

18. Let it sit for a few minutes with the electric pressure cooker lid on before serving to allow the flavours to mix. Serve hot.

Nutrition Facts

Doukhobor Borshch
Per 1 cup (250 mL)

Calories 299

Calories from fat 171

% Daily Value*	
Fat 19 g	29%
Saturated 12 g	75%
Trans 1 g	
Polyunsaturated 1 g	
Monounsaturated 5 g	
Cholesterol 58 mg	19%
Sodium 710 mg	31%
Potassium 820 mg	23%
Carbohydrate 30 g	10%
Fibre 5 g	21%
Sugars 6 g	7%
Protein 5 g	10%
Vitamin A 2,714 iu	54%
Vitamin C 36 mg	44%
Calcium 82 mg	8%
Iron 2 mg	11%

*Percent Daily Values are based on a 2,000-calorie diet.

ELECTRIC PRESSURE COOKER
MATZO BALL SOUP

My electric pressure cooker Matzo Ball Soup recipe is an adaptation of a friend's traditional family recipe. This recipe requires a lot of "spoons" to prepare, even with my adaptation that greatly reduces cook time.

A staple during Passover, matzo has a history that goes back thousands of years. As for when matzo was turned into a dumpling (matzo ball) and added to Jewish chicken soup, also known as "Jewish penicillin," this history is a bit more uncertain.

Some say matzo ball soup became a Passover staple in the 1800s, when Jewish people were a large part of the eastern European fabric. As the story goes, Jewish people started to create these dumplings to fit in with the rest of society. However, this history is largely disputed both by scholars who specialize in eastern European history and by Jewish people themselves.

What is probably closer to reality is the decolonized history. This history states that the tradition of matzo ball soup began in the early 1800s, when the creation of matzo bread became industrialized and anybody could buy the bread, create matzo meal, and turn it into a dumpling. Everyone, Jew and Gentile, began enjoying matzo ball soup once matzo was no longer relegated to being either homemade or purchased from kosher bakeries.

Before the early 1900s eastern Europe was a very multicultural place, with unenforced borders and cultural groups who lived nomadic lives, and people were simply accepted as they were. Eastern Europeans were not divided into ethnic and cultural groups as they were in Western countries and cultures. Eastern Europe was the first true multicultural society, and this dish is a reflection of that. It is also reflective of a people who, for thousands of years, have been forced to pack up their food, flee, and persevere. It is important to note the events that forced Jews out of eastern Europe and into North America, bringing their matzo balls and soup with them. My great-grandparents' journey tells one of these stories. They were forced to hide the fact they were Jewish to immigrate to Canada during partition in the interwar period.

During their escape to North America, their country of origin, Galicia, became no more. At each port of entry along their journey, their nationality would change from Galician to Ukrainian and then to Polish as war and partition carved up their homeland. They weren't allowed to declare themselves as ethnically Ukrainian, as they had identified. Identity and nationality were imposed upon them by each country they entered on their journey.

The borders would move several times as partition continued. When the final lines were drawn, the neighbouring villages from which they came were now on separate sides of a new border between Poland and Ukraine. During the Second World War, these villages ceased to exist, along with the family that did not make it out. My history was lost, as were the traditional Jewish meals, as they lived Christian lives in Canada in order to be accepted. This story once again started to play out at the beginning of 2022 when Russia invaded Ukraine, including the area that was once a country called Galicia.

Food is such an integral part of Jewish culture. It is woven into the fabric of our souls. Some of the more traditional foods, like matzo balls and the soup, take days to prepare. Days on which to prepare food are limited in many Jewish homes. Being disabled compounds this. It's important that these traditions stay alive, that the foods that feed the soul thrive, especially as we still experience the intergenerational trauma that is embedded in our bones as our entire histories and lives have been subjected to repeated acts of genocide and erasure.

Electric Pressure Cooker Matzo Ball Soup

Despite multiple attempts to erase a people and their food, this dish has been served in some form similar to the recipe offered here for generations in families of Ashkenazi Jewish descent.

PREP:	COOK:	NATURAL RELEASE:	TOTAL:
1 hour	1 hour, 25 minutes, over 2 days	20 minutes + 1 full	2 hours, 45 minutes + 1 full natural release, over 2 days

CUISINE:	HEAT INDEX:	STORAGE:	SERVINGS:	CALORIES PER SERVING:
Jewish kosher	None	Freeze, or jar at 11 lb (76 kPa) of pressure for 75 minutes	8 × 2 cups (500 mL)	376 kcal

Gather Equipment:

- 6-quart (5.68 L) electric pressure cooker
- 3-quart (2.84 L) electric pressure cooker
- Cutting board
- Knife
- Measuring cups and spoons
- Spice ball, cheesecloth, tea bag, or anything to make a spice pouch
- Slotted ladle
- Fine-mesh strainer
- Lots of stainless steel mixing bowls
- Electric hand mixer or stand mixer
- Trivet
- Wooden spoon

Prepare and Mise en Place Ingredients:

Matzo Ball Soup Stock: Day 1

- 6 sprigs fresh parsley (with stems)
- 3 sprigs fresh thyme
- 1 tablespoon (15 mL) whole black peppercorns
- 8 cups (2 L) water
- 1.36 kg (3 lb) chicken pieces (can be a mix of backs and feet if you can get them, a leftover roast chicken carcass, or skin-on chicken wings)
- 4 medium carrots, peeled, trimmed, and cut in thirds
- 2 large stalks celery, cut in thirds
- 1 leek, cleaned, trimmed, and cut in 7.5 cm (3-inch) slices
- 1 medium yellow onion, peeled, trimmed, and studded with 16 whole cloves

Prepare and Mise en Place Ingredients:

Matzo Balls: Days 1–2

- 4 large eggs
- 1 tablespoon (15 mL) dried dill, or 2 tablespoons (30 mL) chopped fresh dill
- 1 tablespoon (15 mL) dried parsley, or 2 tablespoons (30 mL) chopped fresh parsley
- 1 tablespoon (15 mL) melted unsalted butter, or 2 tablespoons (30 mL) fat from the chicken stock
- 1 teaspoon (5 mL) salt (or kosher salt)
- ⅛ teaspoon (pinch) onion powder
- ¾ cup (180 mL) Matzo Meal (page 60)
- 2 cups (500 mL) Matzo Ball Soup stock (set aside after making the stock)
- 2 cups (500 mL) water

Prepare and Mise en Place Ingredients:

Matzo Ball Soup: Day 2

- 900 grams (2 lb) boneless skinless chicken thighs, cut in quarters
- 1 teaspoon (5 mL) salt (or kosher salt)
- Black pepper to taste
- 4 medium carrots, peeled and cut in small cubes
- 4 large stalks celery, cut in small cubes
- 4 parsnips, peeled and cut in small cubes
- 2 medium yellow onions, peeled, trimmed, and studded with 8 whole cloves each
- 6 sprigs fresh parsley (with stems)
- 3 sprigs fresh thyme
- 1 tablespoon (15 mL) whole black peppercorns, in a spice ball
- 1 tablespoon (15 mL) salt (or kosher salt)
- Fresh dill for serving

Tip: Do not freeze or jar the soup with the matzo balls. Freeze those separately, or just enjoy them as a snack before the end of 3 days' storage in the fridge.

INSTRUCTIONS

Matzo Ball Soup Stock: Day 1

1. Put the parsley, thyme, and peppercorns into a spice ball. In a 6-quart (5.68 L) electric pressure cooker, add the water and then all remaining ingredients, starting with the chicken pieces and finishing with the onion.
2. Place and seal the lid. Cook on the Soup setting for 1 hour.
3. If you are doing this on its own day, feel free to let the pressure naturally release. If you want it all done in one day, natural-release pressure for 10 minutes, then use cold, wet cloths on the metal parts of the lid to hurry up the rest of the pressure release. *Do not use the quick-release valve because the stock will spew out of the vent.*
4. Once the pressure has released, remove the lid. Using a slotted ladle, remove all the solids. Compost the onion and leeks. Put the carrots and celery in a dish to save as a snack. Separate the chicken meat from the bones and save it for later use in sandwiches or whatever else you'd like. Compost the bones.
5. Pour the stock through a fine-mesh strainer into a mixing bowl.
6. Set aside 2 cups (500 mL) of the stock for the matzo balls (skip this step if you aren't making matzo balls). Refrigerate both quantities of stock for at least 3 hours so you can easily skim off the fat.

Matzo Balls: Day 1

1. Chill a stainless steel mixing bowl.
2. Once the bowl is chilled, separate the eggs, placing the egg whites in the chilled bowl and the yolks in a separate bowl.
3. Using an electric hand mixer or stand mixer, beat the egg whites until they form stiff peaks. Put them in the fridge to chill until you need them.

4. In the bowl with the egg yolks, add the dill, parsley, melted butter or chicken fat, salt, and onion powder. Mix well.

5. Mix in the Matzo Meal a little at a time, until well combined.

6. Gradually fold in the egg whites, about a quarter of the egg whites at a time, until thoroughly mixed.

7. Cover and refrigerate overnight.

Matzo Balls: Day 2

1. Once the matzo ball mix has chilled and you're ready to make the soup, in a 3-quart (2.84 L) electric pressure cooker, add the 2 cups (500 mL) of stock you set aside, the water, and the trivet.

2. Turn on the electric pressure cooker to Sauté. Heat until the broth and water boils, about 5 minutes.

3. While the stock is heating up, roll the matzo ball mix into 2 cm (¾-inch) balls.

4. Once the stock-and-water mixture is boiling, lightly drop the balls into the pot using a spoon. Make sure the balls are floating and not sticking to the trivet. The trivet is there just in case one falls apart, so it doesn't burn.

5. Press Cancel. Place and seal the lid. Set to High Pressure for 12 minutes.

6. Natural-release pressure for 10 minutes, then quick-release any remaining pressure.

7. Put the cooked matzo balls in a dish and set aside until ready to serve.

8. Save the stock-and-water mix.

Matzo Ball Soup: Day 2

1. In a stainless steel mixing bowl, add the chicken thighs. Sprinkle with 1 teaspoon (5 mL) salt and pepper to taste. Mix well. Refrigerate for at least 30 minutes.

2. Remove the fat from the Matzo Ball Soup stock that was chilling overnight. Freeze the fat for future use.

3. In the 6-quart (5.68 L) electric pressure cooker, add the carrots, celery, parsnips, studded onions, parsley, thyme, the spice ball with the peppercorns, and 1 tablespoon (15 mL) salt.

4. Pour in the Matzo Ball Soup stock.

5. Add the chicken thighs.

6. Place and seal the lid. Cook at High Pressure for 8 minutes.

7. Natural-release all the pressure. *Do not use the quick-release valve because the stock will spew out of the vent.* Use cold wet cloths on the metal parts of the lid to hurry up the rest of the pressure release.

8. Remove the lid. Discard the onions, parsley, thyme, and spice ball. Add the saved stock-and-water mix from step 8 of "Matzo Balls: Day 2" by pouring it through a fine-mesh strainer. (If you didn't make the matzo balls, add 2 cups/500 mL water.)

9. Serve the soup with fresh dill and 1 matzo ball per serving (or double the matzo ball ingredients if you want two!).

Nutrition Facts
Matzo Ball Soup
Per 2 cups (500 mL)

Calories 376

Calories from fat 99	
% Daily Value*	
Fat 11 g	17%
Saturated 4 g	25%
Cholesterol 220 mg	73%
Sodium 1,697 mg	74%
Potassium 974 mg	28%
Carbohydrate 40 g	13%
Fibre 8 g	33%
Sugars 9 g	10%
Protein 29 g	58%
Vitamin A 10,850 iu	217%
Vitamin C 25.8 mg	31%
Calcium 133 mg	13%
Iron 3.6 mg	20%

*Percent Daily Values are based on a 2,000-calorie diet.

ELECTRIC PRESSURE COOKER AND AIR FRYER VEGETARIAN SAMOSAS

Samosa is another one of those foods that say, "I love you." Whenever a celebration is happening, or people are gathered to mourn, or disaster hits, or festival celebrations are being prepared, or people are striking, there is a gurdwara somewhere with its kitchen with an assembly line of people preparing samosa. During the flood of 2021 that cut off much of British Columbia from the rest of Canada, thousands of Sikhs gathered in gurdwaras in the city of Surrey, prepared food, and then rented helicopters to get that food to people stranded in the town of Hope. Part of that food was samosa.

It is labour intensive and soul fulfilling.

It is also an example of a multicultural dish, not only because of how ubiquitous this staple is in many parts of BC and Ontario, but because of how many different varieties exist throughout South Asia. This is thanks to how the food was imported from Persia 800 or more years ago. And it existed for at least 300 years before it was imported.

Regardless of the variety of this dish, it is a labour of love. First you must make the dough. Then you have to make the filling. Then you must cut the dough, with many variations of how to do this. Then you stuff it. Then glue it shut. Finally, you fry it. Hours and hours of laborious love for the perfect bite of warming goodness.

Electric Pressure Cooker and Air Fryer Vegetarian Samosas

While I am not the first person to figure out that using phyllo dough can help make cooking samosa a little more accessible, it is still a highly underutilized trick. When you add my adaptations that allow for cooking using an electric pressure cooker and air fryer, this important staple will remain accessible to all and become re-accessible to many.

PREP:	PRESSURE COOKER:	NATURAL RELEASE:	OVEN-STYLE AIR FRYER:	COMBO-STYLE AIR FRYER:	TOTAL:
20 minutes + 1 hour folding	10 minutes	10 minutes	12–18 minutes	30 minutes	1 hour, 52 minutes–2 hours, 10 minutes

CUISINE:	HEAT INDEX:	STORAGE:	SERVINGS:	CALORIES PER SERVING:
Indian	Mild to medium	Freeze, or refrigerate for up to 3 days	36	91 kcal

Gather Equipment:

- 6-quart (5.68 L) electric pressure cooker
- Oven-style air fryer or 8-quart (7.57 L) electric pressure cooker–air fryer combo
- A second inner pot if using combo cooker
- Dehydration racks (2 tiers) or stackable trivets if using combo cooker
- Trivet
- Steaming basket
- 2 cutting boards
- Knife
- Measuring cups and spoons
- Pastry brush
- Wooden spoon
- Large bowl
- Tongs

Prepare and Mise en Place Ingredients:

- 1 cup (250 mL) water
- 6 medium russet potatoes, diced in 1 cm (⅓-inch) cubes
- 1 cup (250 mL) frozen peas
- 2 tablespoons (30 mL) extra-virgin olive oil
- 1 teaspoon (5 mL) cumin seeds
- 2 medium yellow onions, diced
- 2 teaspoons (10 mL) Ginger-Garlic Masala (page 44)
- 2 teaspoons (10 mL) Thana Jeeroo (page 46)
- 1½ teaspoons (7.5 mL) salt
- 1 teaspoon (5 mL) ground turmeric
- 1 teaspoon (5 mL) ground cayenne pepper
- ¼ cup (60 mL) cilantro, chopped
- 454 g (1 lb) package phyllo pastry dough, defrosted and cut in 4 equal sections
- ¼ cup (60 mL) melted unsalted butter or ghee

INSTRUCTIONS

To prepare the filling:

1. In a 6-quart (5.68 L) electric pressure cooker, add the water and then place the trivet in the inner pot. If using an 8-quart (7.57 L) combo cooker and two inner pots, do this step in the first inner pot.
2. Place the potatoes and peas in the steaming basket. Place the basket on the trivet.
3. Place and seal the lid. Cook at High Pressure for 2 minutes.
4. Natural-release pressure for 10 minutes, then quick-release any remaining pressure.
5. Remove the steaming basket and trivet and set aside.
6. Empty the water and place the inner pot back into the cooker.
7. Turn the electric pressure cooker on to Sauté. When it's hot, add the olive oil and cumin seeds. Sauté until fragrant, about 30 seconds.
8. Add the onions and Ginger-Garlic Masala. Sauté until the onions start to brown, about 6–7 minutes.
9. Press Cancel.
10. While still hot, add the cooked potatoes and peas, Thana Jeeroo, salt, turmeric, and cayenne pepper. Combine well.
11. Remove the inner pot from the cooker. Stir in the cilantro.
12. Put the filling into a large bowl for easier access when filling the samosas.

To fold the samosas:

1. Carefully grab one sectioned sheet of phyllo dough and place it flat on a surface. I like to use a wooden cutting board to fold samosas.
2. Add approximately 2 tablespoons (30 mL) of filling to the bottom corner of the dough.
3. Fold it into a triangle, following the instructions on the back of the phyllo dough package.
4. Grab a second sectioned sheet of dough.
5. Place the already folded samosa on the bottom of this sheet and fold again, using the triangle instructions.
6. Use the melted butter or ghee to seal the edge, then lightly brush the entire samosa with it.
7. Repeat steps 1–6 until all the samosas are folded. **Note:** Once you have 12 samosas folded, you can begin air frying. In the time it takes you to air fry one batch, you should be able to finish folding the next batch.

If using an oven-style air fryer:

1. Using the Bake function, set to 375°F (190°C) for 3 minutes. Let the oven preheat.
2. Place 12 prepared samosas on one of the racks. Be careful to leave a small gap between each samosa. Once the Add Food indicator goes off, place the rack on the bottom rung of the oven.
3. Cook 2–3 minutes until the tops are golden brown.
4. Flip the samosas. Using the same setting, cook for another 2–3 minutes until both sides are golden brown.
5. Remove the samosas.
6. Repeat steps 1–5 until all the samosas are cooked.

If using an electric pressure cooker–air fryer combo:

1. Using the second inner pot, place the bottom tier of the stacking trivets into the inner pot. Place 6 prepared samosas on that trivet, making sure to leave space between each samosa.

2. Place the second tier of the stacking trivet on top of the first tier. Place 6 prepared samosas on that trivet, making sure to leave space between each samosa.

3. Place the air fryer lid. Air fry on the Bake setting at 375°F (190°C) for 6 minutes.

4. Remove the lid. Take out the top layer of samosas and remove that rack.

5. Flip the bottom layer of samosas. Replace the top rack and return the removed samosas, making sure to flip them.

6. Place the air fryer lid. Air fry on the Bake setting at 375°F (190°C) for 4 minutes.

7. Remove the samosas.

8. Repeat steps 1–7 until all the samosas are cooked.

Nutrition Facts
Vegetarian Samosa
Per 1 samosa

Calories 91
Calories from fat 27

% Daily Value*

Fat 3 g	5%
Saturated 1 g	6%
Trans 1 g	
Polyunsaturated 1 g	
Monounsaturated 1 g	
Cholesterol 3 mg	1%
Sodium 161 mg	7%
Potassium 183 mg	5%
Carbohydrate 14 g	5%
Fibre 1 g	4%
Sugars 1 g	1%
Protein 2 g	4%
Vitamin A 103 iu	2%
Vitamin C 4 mg	5%
Calcium 11 mg	1%
Iron 1 mg	6%

*Percent Daily Values are based on a 2,000-calorie diet.

APPENDIX

HOW TO MEAL PLAN AND PREP FOR SURGERY RECOVERY

Planning for post-operative recovery and care is stressful. In my experience, it's more stressful than the surgery itself. Your miles—or kilometres—may vary. You need to plan for six weeks, at minimum, that you won't be able to do many tasks. This can be for a variety of reasons, including post-op instructions and/or all your "spoons" being dedicated to recovery and pain management. You may not have a lot of physical support during this time. You could also have great supports, but the less everyone needs to do during this period, the better.

There is a reason that people bring over food during times of stress. Cooking tends to become the most demanding thing during times of recovery, not just post-op recovery but also big life changes that lead to stress, like a loved one dying. Most of the time, you can't plan for periods of grief. However, you can plan for those times when meeting the most basic need for food will be compromised. Knowing where to start, and how, can be overwhelming. I'm overwhelmed writing this, and I've done it many times.

The biggest hurdle for me when it comes to planning in general is knowing where to start. If you start at the wrong place, reaching your goal can become impossible. When I planned for my first six-week-minimum recovery, I sat down with a pen and a notebook. The rest of the steps can be easily changed to fit your needs and disabilities.

Step 1: As soon as you receive an approximate time frame for surgery, pick seven or eight favourite recipes. You don't want to pick too many recipes because the more you choose, the more difficult it becomes to prepare a cooking timetable and get everything cooked before the deadline. I have seven go-to meals for surgery recovery: Butter Chicken, Chicken Korma, Thai Coconut Chicken Soup (recipe available on *Disabled Kitchen and Garden* blog at disabledkitchenandgarden.ca), Doukhobor Borshch, Effin' Good Chili, Chicken Stew, and Asian Fusion Chicken.

Step 2: Chart how many batches of each you need to cook. I like to do this in a physical notebook, but you could also do it in a spreadsheet or whatever other method works for your brain and disabilities. When I chart out my meals, it's a written version of the following:

POST-OP MEAL PLAN—6 WEEKS

Butter Chicken	× 2	= 15 meals
Chicken Korma	× 1	= 16 meals
Thai Coconut Chicken Soup	× 2	= 10 meals
Borshch	× 1	= 6 meals
Chili	× 4	= 9 meals (with 9 for partner)
Chicken Stew	× 2	= 12 meals
Asian Fusion Chicken	× 4	= 16 meals
		= 42 lunches and 42 suppers

Step 3: Figure out what you need to make and store everything. Once I've figured out exactly what I need to cook, I figure out what I need to cook it and store it. Again, I write it all out in my handy-dandy notebook. But you can use whatever method works for you. I create two separate lists. One list is what I need to store everything. The other list is a rough outline of all the ingredients, including quantities, that I will need to buy so that I can better budget for all the extra cooking.

Here is an example from surgery planning I wrote a few years ago:

CANNING NEEDS

Needed 500 mL jars	= 93
Current empty jars on hand	= 16
Need to buy	= 77
	= 7 cases of 12

If you have a big chest freezer and plan to freeze all the meals, then plan for freezer containers instead of canning jars. You don't want to include jars/containers currently holding food in your on-hand numbers. You need those to hold the food you're going to eat leading up to surgery.

You will have a lot of extra jars/containers after your recovery period is over, but they will get filled up quickly if you follow my "How to Meal Prep" steps (page 20), making planning for surgery next time less work.

PRIMARY SHOPPING LIST

4.9 kg boneless skinless chicken thighs	4 roasting chickens	3.6 kg lean ground beef
12 × 398 mL cans diced tomatoes	6 × 400 mL cans coconut milk	Unsalted butter
Celery	Carrots	24 potatoes
Thyme (if not growing in my Aero-Garden)	Rosemary	Beet
Sage (if not growing in my Aero-Garden)	4 green peppers	Cilantro (if not growing in my Aero-Garden)
1 × 796 mL crushed tomatoes	Bags of onions	Parsley (if not growing in my Aero-Garden)
Garlic	236 mL whipping cream	Ginger
Chicken broth	Greek yogourt	6 cans tomato paste
Almonds	Dill (if not growing in my AeroGarden)	4 × 796 mL dark kidney beans
4 bags mixed bell peppers	4 × 398 mL can San Marzano tomatoes	4 × 398 mL fire-roasted tomatoes
Green onions	4 lemons	Beef bouillon cubes

There are many other ingredients needed for each recipe that are not on the primary shopping list. That's because my pantry organizing and shopping list scheme is such that those ingredients are always on hand in abundance. This is what will be needed in addition to my normal shopping list.

Step 4: Make a cooking schedule and weekly shopping lists. If you read the "How to Meal Plan" chapter, then you know I meal plan in broad strokes a month ahead instead of making precise weekly meal plans. That changes when I have surgery coming up. When I have an upcoming surgery, I take my list from step 2 and figure out what I need to cook each week while planning to cook specifically for surgery four times per week.

Cooking that many times a week can be impossible. But with everything clearly laid out, someone can take my plan and easily do some of that cooking, shopping, and food storage for me. The following is an example of how this looked when I was planning for surgery cooking through the end of April and May 2019:

COOKING SCHEDULE—WEEK 1	
April 16	Cook Butter Chicken × 1
April 18	Cook Butter Chicken × 1
April 20	Cook Chicken Korma
April 21	Cook Roast Chicken and freeze carcass

APRIL 14 SURGERY SHOPPING LIST	
Roasting chicken	Onions (2 bags)
Unsalted butter	Family pack chicken thighs × 2
Basmati rice × 2	Parsley
Almonds	Lemon
Potatoes × 6	

COOKING SCHEDULE—WEEK 2	
April 23	Thai Coconut Chicken Soup
April 25	Chicken Stew
April 27	Borshch
April 28	Cook Roast Chicken and freeze carcass

APRIL 21 SURGERY SHOPPING LIST	
Roasting chicken	Large freezer bags
Thyme	Beet
236 mL whipping cream	Potatoes × 8
Thai red curry paste	1 L chicken broth
Lemon	Lime juice
Green onions	Family pack chicken breasts
Rosemary	1 green pepper
Crushed tomatoes	Celery
Dill	

COOKING SCHEDULE—WEEK 3	
April 30	Chicken Stew
May 2	Chili
May 4	Chili
May 5	Cook Roast Chicken and freeze carcass

APRIL 28 SURGERY SHOPPING LIST	
Roasting chicken	Worcestershire sauce
Lemon	Unsalted butter
2 red bell peppers	2 green bell peppers
Serrano peppers (tray)	Garlic
4 × 398 mL San Marzano tomatoes	4 × 796 mL dark kidney beans
Beef bouillon cubes	Potatoes × 6
1.8 kg lean ground beef	Jalapenos × 6
6 × 398 mL diced tomatoes	4 × 398 mL fire-roasted tomatoes

COOKING SCHEDULE—WEEK 4	
May 6	Asian Fusion Chicken
May 7	Asian Fusion Chicken
May 9	Thai Coconut Chicken Soup
May 11	Chili
May 12	Cook Roast Chicken and freeze carcass

MAY 4 SURGERY SHOPPING LIST	
Roasting chicken	Celery
Lemon	Family pack chicken thighs × 3
Bag of onions × 2	Potatoes × 4
Unsalted butter	Rosemary
Parsley	400 mL coconut milk
Ginger	Garlic
Thai red curry paste	Thyme
900 g lean ground beef	Soy sauce
Dill	

COOKING SCHEDULE—WEEK 5	
May 14	Asian Fusion Chicken
May 16	Asian Fusion Chicken
May 18	Chili

MAY 11 SURGERY SHOPPING LIST	
Family pack chicken thighs × 1	900 g lean ground beef
Serrano peppers	Garlic
Jalapenos × 2	Ginger

Step 5: Follow the plan. This may appear obvious, but I have often found myself second-guessing my food choices when preparing for surgery. I'm always worried that when it's time to eat, there will be nothing I want to eat. The reality always turns out to be different. Often, I'm so tired that I don't care what I eat and tell my partner to warm up anything. And the odd time I'm not feeling any of my choices, we order in.

To carry out this plan, don't forget to reach out and ask for help when you need it. And if you find yourself without the "spoons" or help to finish the best-laid plans, there is no failure or shame in filling grocery deliveries with ready-made meals as you recover.

GROCERY LIST

PRODUCE	MEATS + SEAFOOD

DAIRY	PANTRY

SNACKS	MISC.

MEAL PLANNER WITH EXAMPLES

WEEK ONE	NOTES
MONDAY: Dog food–making day TUESDAY: Shop WEDNESDAY: THURSDAY: Dog food–making day FRIDAY: SATURDAY: Food delivery and staples prep SUNDAY: Dog food–making day	Let's try for some borshch and butter chicken this week

WEEK TWO	NOTES
MONDAY: TUESDAY: Shop WEDNESDAY: Dog food–making day THURSDAY: FRIDAY: SATURDAY: Dog food–making day/Food delivery SUNDAY:	Let's try for some Mexican Casserole, Chicken Biryani and Thai Green Curry this week

WEEK THREE	NOTES
MONDAY: TUESDAY: Dog food–making day/Shop WEDNESDAY: THURSDAY: FRIDAY: Dog food–making day SATURDAY: Food delivery and staples prep SUNDAY:	Don't need to cook because I have enough premade meals but if I have the spoons, let's try for some Matzo Ball Soup

WEEK FOUR	NOTES
MONDAY: Dog food–making day TUESDAY: Shop WEDNESDAY: THURSDAY: Dog food–making day FRIDAY: SATURDAY: Food delivery SUNDAY: Dog food–making day	Let's try for some chili and spaghetti

MEAL PLANNER

WEEK ONE	NOTES
MONDAY:	
TUESDAY:	
WEDNESDAY:	
THURSDAY:	
FRIDAY:	
SATURDAY:	
SUNDAY:	

WEEK TWO	NOTES
MONDAY:	
TUESDAY:	
WEDNESDAY:	
THURSDAY:	
FRIDAY:	
SATURDAY:	
SUNDAY:	

WEEK THREE	NOTES
MONDAY:	
TUESDAY:	
WEDNESDAY:	
THURSDAY:	
FRIDAY:	
SATURDAY:	
SUNDAY:	

WEEK FOUR	NOTES
MONDAY:	
TUESDAY:	
WEDNESDAY:	
THURSDAY:	
FRIDAY:	
SATURDAY:	
SUNDAY:	

ACKNOWLEDGEMENTS

Thank you to my partner, Andrew, for being my assistant during COVID-19 and walking into the kitchen and studio with stacks of dirty dishes, cleaning them, and putting them away. Also, thank you for never doubting I could do this and supporting this project from day one. Thank you to my children, Caleb and Tristan, for the constant encouragement and support. Thank you to John for writing the foreword and being the reason I learned about Urvashi Pitre and the good things about Instant Pot.

Thank you to Danya for trusting me with her family's Matzo Ball Soup recipe. Thank you to Roopa for trusting me with her story. Thank you to Mae for teaching Tristan how to cook Thai food, for sharing those recipes with me, and for trusting I would stay true to them as I developed pressure cooker versions for this cookbook. Thank you to the Thiara family for making me one of their own and teaching me everything I know about Panjabi cooking. Thank you to every person who shared their food and cultures with me. Thank you to the many food historians who filled my knowledge gaps.

Thank you to all the local farmers who are part of the Cow-Op for making it that much easier to buy local to create the best food and imagery possible. Thank you to Economic Development Cowichan for sponsoring my Island Good membership, which helped to grow my brand.

Thank you to my beta readers, recipe testers, friends, readers of *Disabled Kitchen and Garden*, and the Pubbers for invaluable feedback and requests that helped to make this book more accessible. Thank you to so many people in the publishing world whose feedback helped me to create a saleable query letter and proposal: Eric Smith, Stacey Graham, Maria Rogers, and Jess Dallow. Thank you to Amy Giuffrida for going beyond, which gave me the affirmation to keep going.

Thank you to my editor Kate Kennedy for being there from the moment I queried and helping to make sure this book is the best version of my vision, in which all at TouchWood Editions so firmly believed and supported. Thank you to my copy editor Meg Yamamoto for catching all the things I could never catch because of executive function issues and aphasia, and for handling my voice with care and respect.

Thank you to publisher Tori Elliott for purchasing my book and for an amazing "call"; for championing my book alongside Kate at various steps along the way to the printer. Thank you to my publicist Curtis Samuel for allowing me to put on my former marketer and publicist hat, and to work with you to ensure people who need this book become aware of it. Thank you to my interior designer Sydney Barnes for taking my design suggestions and vision and making them a million times better; for taking the time to research neurodivergent-friendly design and implementing what you learned. Thank you to my cover designer Jazmin Welch for creating an amazing text-based cover that has so much impact. Thank you to my proofreader Senica Maltese for catching all the things that inevitably sneak in and need fixing. Thank you to owner of TouchWood Editions Pat Touchie for continuing your strong commitment to BC publishing and historically excluded voices.

I acknowledge the support of the Canada Council for the Arts.

INDEX

NOTES

NOTES

NOTES

NOTES

NOTES

NOTES

ABOUT THE AUTHOR

Based in Duncan, BC, Jules Sherred works as a commercial food photographer and stylist, author and recipe developer, journalist, and outspoken advocate for disability and trans rights. He is an official contributor to Getty Images, a staff writer for Fstoppers news site, has been a guest speaker at photography conferences, and is an instructor in Andrew Scrivani's food photography academy.

Locally Jules works in partnership with Cowichan Farm and Food Hub to create and deliver programming to help combat food insecurity in the Cowichan Valley. He is also a steering committee member, and research lead for the Cowichan Food Policy project.

In 2022, Jules photographed and produced *Nourish: A Celebration*, an art exhibit at the Cowichan Valley Arts Council that celebrated local food and beverage producers, farmers, vineyards, and the restaurants that kept people fed during COVID-19 in the face of impossible circumstances, including multiple climate change disasters.

Consulting on policy and legislation at multiple levels of government in regard to transgender human rights issues, Jules has written about his personal experiences as a survivor of conversion practices, and specifically advocated for improvements to legislative bans in order to encompass practices targeting trans people and identities.

Jules's food blog *Disabled Kitchen and Garden* was born out of the need to include disabled people in the conversation around food. Through the site, he shares the benefits and joys of accessible products while providing a number of tips, tricks, and recipes to make cooking and gardening easier for a variety of disabilities. You can find Jules online at disabledkitchenandgarden.ca, polariscreative.ca, and julessherred.com.